A perspective from leaders at McKinsey & Company

Fast Times

How digital winners set direction, learn, and adapt

Fast Times

How digital winners set direction, learn, and adapt

Arun Arora
Peter Dahlstrom
Klemens Hjartar
Florian Wunderlich

amazon publishing

Published by Amazon Publishing, Seattle
www.apub.com

Amazon, the Amazon logo, and Amazon Publishing
are trademarks of Amazon.com, Inc., or its affiliates.

ISBN-13: 9781542007696
ISBN-10: 1542007690

Cover design by Magdalena Jusko

Printed in the United States of America
First edition

Acknowledgments

We want to thank the following people, whose expertise and dedication were crucial in helping us to produce this book:

Pierce Groover
Former Associate Partner in McKinsey's Chicago office

Magdalena Jusko
Design Director in McKinsey's San Francisco office

Hamza Khan
Partner in McKinsey's London office

Mary Kuntz
Senior Editor

Joanne Mason
Senior Editor

Andrea Peyracchia
Partner in McKinsey's Milan office

Josh Rosenfield
Senior Editor in McKinsey's New York office

Elin Sandnes
Partner in McKinsey's Oslo office

Barr Seitz
Executive Editor in McKinsey's New York office

Hayk Yegoryan
Engagement Manager in McKinsey's Amsterdam office

Additionally, we would like to acknowledge our McKinsey colleagues for their insights and guidance in this undertaking:

Said Abouali, Varun Atre, Christian Behrends, Michael Bender, Emilio Capela, Alex Cappy, Anna Checa, Andrea Del Miglio, Claudio Feser, Daniel Glaser, Julie Goran, Nicolaus Henke, Martin Bech Holte, Laura LaBerge, Kevin Laczkowski, Mike Newborn, Anand Rao, Daniel Rona, Indy Saha, Bill Schaninger, Saravana Sivanandham, Nick van Damm, Paul Willmott, and Paul Yuan

We would also like to thank our friends from Korn Ferry:

Neil Griffiths, Melissa Swift, Fiona Vickers, and Jason Waterman

What this book is about

First movers win. That's the hard reality of the digital age. Our research is clear on this point. You have to be first at delivering something that has value and do it at sufficient scale—whether that's a new product, a new platform, or superior customer service—to streak ahead of the competition. While adopting a fast-follower strategy can help you stay in the game, it's risky. Time and again we see companies that have taken a fast-follower strategy not be able to move fast enough.

To be first, you have to be fast, of course. Speed matters. Speed, however, is an outcome of deliberate actions and behaviors, and not the source of competitive advantage in itself. And the most important actions and behaviors to develop are those that help a company set the right direction, and then learn and adapt faster than anyone else.

That's because disruptions are constantly upending the business landscape. Without being able to learn and adapt faster than the competition, businesses run the risk of losing out on the next wave of disruption. Speed only makes sense, though, if you're going in the right direction.

Digital winners have an adaptive learning engine at the core of their organization. They are deliberate in developing the technology, analytics, capabilities, and people to spot value, test ideas with customers, and adapt quickly to what they learn.

Developing this learn-and-adapt capability should be the goal of every digital transformation. *Fast Times* highlights the most important actions companies can take to set a strong strategic direction, then learn and adapt faster than the competition. ∎

Who should read this book

This book is for senior executives who are frustrated by the slow pace and limited return on investment (ROI) of their digital transformations, and are unsure what's holding them back.

We wrote *Fast Times* based on our personal experiences leading dozens of digital programs for leaders who want to quickly understand what really matters in a digital transformation. For this reason, we focused this book on the handful of actions that experience has shown have an outsize impact on results in terms of speed and value.

To help highlight what those actions are—and make it easy to find the most relevant content—we organized *Fast Times* around a set of the most critical questions for executives to answer.

Fast Times is not for everyone. It doesn't offer a comprehensive blueprint for a digital transformation. Nor does it address why a digital transformation is necessary—we wrote this book for executives who already understand this necessity and have embarked on their transformation journeys. This book will also be less useful to C-suite executives and board members who are at the end of their tenure and so will not have the time needed to implement many of our recommendations.

This book is for leaders at companies where digital transformation is a top-three priority. We hope *Fast Times* will help executives think differently about what they are trying to achieve so they can break through the problems they encounter and accelerate the transformation of their companies. ∎

At a glance

Everything about a digital transformation should be focused on how a company can set the right direction, and then learn and adapt faster than their current—and future—competitors. This can be complicated and therefore challenging. Experience has shown that bearing in mind a number of crucial truths can help make a digital transformation successful:

Transforming into a winning digital organization is a bigger commitment than most people think.

In 2014, Joe Lacob, the Silicon Valley venture capitalist and owner of the Golden State Warriors basketball team, made a huge decision. He let go of Mark Jackson, the coach who had rebuilt the Warriors and taken them from obscurity to the playoffs. Lacob realized that to win championships, being good wasn't good enough. So he gambled a good team for the chance to build a great team that could win championships. And he succeeded. The Warriors won three championships in the following four years.

That kind of ambition and commitment is missing at many companies today. They have made significant progress with digital initiatives, but many of them have stalled in "pilot purgatory," unable to sustain and scale the benefits. Having bold aspirations matters, but only when also matched by corresponding commitment. Without allocating funds and resources at sufficient scale over enough time, the value of digital will remain a mirage—promising but forever out of reach.

What does that commitment look like? Our research has shown that winning companies exceed laggards in both the magnitude and the scope of their digital investments. We know that incumbent companies that invest triple the amount of their peers in new technologies are more likely to acquire digital companies, and are willing to cannibalize their own core business to achieve revenue growth that's two and a half times that of the laggards.[1]

This level of commitment means upending your HR processes to find and train the right talent. It means modernizing—even rebuilding—IT systems so that they are modular and flexible enough to test new products or services, and adapt quickly. It means embedding advanced analytics in processes across the entire organization to accelerate, automate, and improve decisions. It means creating new processes and performance management systems to support a culture that learns and adapts. And it means deploying your best people and resources for the transformation over the long haul . . . no matter what.

Speed comes from balancing when to go fast and when to slow down.

Success requires the ambidexterity to be both fast and slow—and knowing when to be which. Running in the wrong direction is worse than standing still. While that might seem obvious, the pressure that executives feel to act fast can be overwhelming. That often leads to frenetic activity and poor decision-making, which in turn leads to rework, cost overruns, delays, or, worst of all, a failed business. Without the combination of thoughtful deliberation and adaptive execution, companies risk having speed without direction.

For that reason, it's crucial to take your time to do certain things right. That starts with investing the time to understand where the business value lies both inside and outside of your organization. Large companies can often free up substantial pools of money, for example, by understanding how every process across the entire organization can be digitized or improved with data and advanced analytics. At the same time, winning companies are paranoid and constantly looking outside their business to understand trends, examine unmet customer needs, and spot inefficiencies in the marketplace. Based on this thinking, you can understand your options, clarify the problem you really need to solve, and figure out how to solve it.

Since a digital transformation is so complex, it's also important to take some time to determine what you want your operating model to be—essentially, how it's all supposed to work so the change can last. As companies shift to working in agile teams organized around discrete processes, products, or customer segments, leaders need to figure out where those people sit, whom they report to, what talent and systems they need, and a myriad of other organizational things. What those are exactly will change over the course of the transformation, of course. But

spending the time to plot out what that adaptive learning engine actually looks like allows leaders to anticipate what capabilities and people to develop so they can speed the transformation.

Only when the deliberate thinking is done does it make sense to hit the gas. That's when teams kick into a cycle of rapid development, experimentation, and iteration across a range of initiatives. Small teams, working in short sprints, across organizational boundaries release minimum viable products, test how they perform in real life, and adapt to what they learn in a constant cycle of continuous improvement. And the wins should come fast. We've seen teams as small as three people unlock millions of dollars in just days and weeks.

You're only as good as your talent.

Talent has always been important to business, but the impact of technology and the challenges of adapting and learning quickly have placed a premium on people. Talent is a significant accelerator of change. But more important than finding all the people you need is finding the right people. Top technical and digital practitioners are up to 10 times more productive than average peers. And the best tend to attract the best, creating a pull for top talent.

Finding these people—data scientists, product owners, agile coaches, designers, data engineers—is a challenge that requires businesses to reinvent their HR function to be both clearer about what kind of talent is needed and more inventive about how to get it. The best HR teams work closely with a digital transformation office to plan for future talent needs as well. Too often companies have promising initiatives die on the vine when the talent pipeline can't keep up.

Just because you want the best, though, doesn't mean they want you. Investing in your brand and a truly compelling employee value proposition—clear career paths, projects that have real impact, inspirational missions, the ability to work on cutting-edge software—is what top talent demands.

For all the new hiring that's necessary, however, the truth is that companies will still need to reskill thousands of members of their existing workforce. The best learning organizations have invested in learning journeys for their people so they continue to grow. Effective learning is a potent mix of classroom training and on-the-job learning supported by technology. These leading businesses tailor learning to the individual, harness technology to deliver a learning asset when and where it's needed, and give people opportunities to try new roles where they can learn new skills on the job.

Harness the duo of soft and hard skills: Culture and technology.

According to McKinsey research, culture is the number one barrier to digital effectiveness. The core component of a successful learning culture is agility—small, cross-functional teams working together to test, learn, and iterate in rapid cycles. But for agile to be effective, people need to believe it's safe to fail. Rewarding noble failures and giving people better tools so they have the confidence to make their own decisions can help. Leaders need to support that safe and flexible learning environment with stable support elements: from agile budgeting and performance management to a total focus on the customer that unifies the organization.

The ability to translate digital into value also requires technology and data that are as flexible and responsive as the people using them. That's nearly impossible with the aging technology leviathans that weigh most large companies down. They're costly and cumbersome to maintain, let alone to integrate with digital solutions.

That's changing. The expansion of cloud technologies, new microservice architectures, and highly automated software creation and deployment processes is fundamentally challenging some long-held beliefs about best practices in technology. These developments have made it possible to pursue end-to-end IT and data platform renewal much more quickly and cheaply than has ever been possible before.

Companies cannot, however, outsource their way to technology renewal. The demands of rapid iteration require companies to bring the necessary capabilities in-house. Winning companies take a "build-it-here" approach and have developers who are comfortable handling code to continuously mold solutions. And they deliberately address one potential source of massive damage—cyber risk—by making it a core part of their transformation program rather than a control function.

Learning has to happen everywhere, all the time.

If the key to business survival were to be boiled down to one acronym, it might be ABL—always be learning. Learning is a core survival skill. "Our customers' needs evolve and grow, so continuous learning is an imperative for all Amazonians," said Beth Galetti, Amazon's head of HR.

For executives, this idea starts with learning what's happening both inside and outside their own companies. They tend to have a hazy sense of their own performance and health, and a dangerously incomplete understanding of what's happening in the marketplace. That's a toxic combination. Only a program dedicated to developing a much clearer view of where you and your competitors stand can help leaders know what to do. In many cases, the value of actually going outside the four walls of the business and seeing what great looks like matters more than anything else.

On the front lines, learning happens by constantly experimenting. Teams learn what works and what doesn't, then build off it. To support this approach, the best companies put in place a learning infrastructure and dedicated process so that it's easy to both access knowledge and share learning. In fact, companies that have implemented digital tools to make information more accessible, such as collaboration platforms, were twice as likely to report successful transformations as companies that didn't.

Learning isn't just for the front lines. Executives themselves should be on the hook for learning as well. The importance of learning plays out particularly in the realm of technology. Tech is an integral part of any true digital transformation, which means executives must become as comfortable with technology as they are with more familiar topics such as finance.

If all of this sounds like a tall order, remember that large companies have massive advantages: a strong brand; an established customer base; experience running large, complex businesses; and access to capital. Remember, too, that learning and adapting are ultimately a mind-set. It's never too late to commit yourself and your organization to learning.

Consider the words of one of the most accomplished artists of all time, Michelangelo, when he was eighty-eight years old: "I'm still learning." ∎

STRATEGY

Are you rushing your strategy–and slowing your transformation?

1

Crafting a deliberate strategy that unlocks real value may take a bit longer at the outset, but can massively accelerate your transformation down the road.

Speed without purpose is just meaningless activity. Nowhere is that truer than in developing a strategy to further your digital transformation. Speed in this case is an outcome of deliberate actions and behaviors. It takes time to identify opportunity and map a path forward, but doing so with care will enable you to move much faster later. Going in the right direction with open eyes and adequate preparation will always be faster than moving at lightning speed in the wrong direction.

The digital age hasn't changed strategy's primary purpose: identifying value and figuring out how to go after it. But *what* the sources of value are and *how* to formulate and execute strategy have changed. Understanding what that means can be the difference between a digital strategy that generates value and one that generates headaches.

In our experience, however, companies just don't spend enough time understanding exactly what value their strategy is meant to capture. Too often the value goal is based on a faulty understanding of market forces or customer needs, or on insufficient analysis.

"Investing time up front to understand where you are going is the only way to be able to move fast," said John Markus Lervik, the CEO of Cognite, a start-up established by Norwegian energy company Aker BP. The company had seen a clear business opportunity in accessing and using data to drive large-scale improvements and greater collaboration. But leaders there weren't sure how to go after it. So rather than rush ahead, they spent six months figuring out the options.

Hitting the pause button turned out to be a smart move. Aker BP's leaders initially thought they'd work with an external provider, but after refining their vision and interviewing potential partners, they realized that none had all the capabilities they needed. This was a crucial insight that saved enormous amounts of time and money that would have been wasted pursuing a doomed strategy. "Only by spending enough time to really understand the problem could we realize that," said Lervik. Instead of going outside, they launched their own business, Cognite, which has quickly become a leading data solutions business across four sectors in Europe.

To unlock the full potential of your digital transformation, you need to be purposeful and deliberate in working at two levels. First, you must be diligent in mapping and executing against all the many big and small actions you can take to improve your current operations. At the same time, you need to identify and take on bold new initiatives that open up vast new opportunities.

Find the value in your own organization

To set a meaningful strategy that will yield the greatest possible gains, you need to map every corner and facet of the organization, looking for opportunities to enhance performance through digital means by doing things better, faster, and more efficiently. You're looking for both top-line and bottom-line opportunities. It's not unlike the process your company may have gone through in earlier periods to find improvements through lean or offshoring.

These opportunities could include automating processes, adding an online channel, simplifying technology, or gathering more granular data on customers to improve cross-selling. One pharma company found that by using advanced analytics it could improve its process for selecting sites for clinical trials, which helped it to reduce enrollment time of patients by 15 percent and reduce overall costs by 10–15 percent.

A telecom company that went through this exercise found the potential for an estimated 25–50 percent gain in EBITDA by bringing digital capabilities to bear across the organization. The opportunities ranged from a 1 percent gain through automating customer service to a 15 percent gain from applying advanced analytics in running the network.

Do you have an ecosystem strategy?[2]

$60 trillion
Revenue potential of ecosystems by 2025

7 of 12
Number of world's largest companies powered by ecosystems today

3%
Portion of incumbent companies with an offensive platform strategy

AI and advanced analytics are particularly rich veins to address for finding potential value. McKinsey analysis has shown that the potential value of these two technologies is $9.5–$15.5 trillion across all sectors. A significant portion of that value comes from improving what companies already do, but capturing that means taking the time to see where AI and advanced analytics can have the greatest impact. In the consumer packaged goods sector, the main source of value is in supply chain management (through improved forecasting, for example) and manufacturing (including practices such as yield, energy, and throughput management as well as inventory and parts optimization). In insurance and retail, the biggest source of AI and advanced analytics value is in marketing and sales practices (such as optimizing pricing and promotions, and managing customer service).[3]

The opportunity in AI and advanced analytics is worth paying special attention to since McKinsey has observed that only a small fraction of the value has been unlocked—as little as 10 percent in some sectors. And McKinsey's AI Index reveals that the gap between leaders and laggards in successful AI and analytics adoption is growing.[4]

As obvious as this approach might seem, our experience has shown that companies often have only a hazy view of how much value they can squeeze out of what they already do. Overcoming this requires a systematic approach to identifying value and the expertise to understand what's even possible with digital and analytics.

Be bold in going after value outside your business

Digital also offers potential avenues for entirely new game-changing initiatives, but to find them, companies need to be as systematic in mapping the value as they are when looking for opportunities to improve what is already in place. The best companies are excellent at identifying unmet needs that are big and sustainable enough to be worth the effort. By both understanding the unique value you deliver to customers and looking for new, tech-enabled ways of delivering that value, you can uncover new business models and product areas for serving customers that could eventually remake your business.

The 150-year-old Deutsche Post DHL Group, the German postal and delivery service, wanted to develop electric vehicles for its delivery vans that would enable it to make deliveries faster and more efficiently. But it couldn't find any manufacturer willing to partner with it. So in 2014 it decided to buy a small start-up called StreetScooter, which already built electric vans. This helped Deutsche Post greatly accelerate the development of an entirely new capability. Deutsche Post reports that some 6,000 of its e-vehicles have driven 26 million kilometers so far in the first few years. The company has opened up a second plant to double its production capacity.[5]

That boldness Deutsche Post DHL Group displayed in moving into developing electric vans is a key characteristic of successful strategies. It's not enough to spot the opportunities; companies need to be aggressive in going after them.

John Deere provides another good example. It transformed itself from a farm-equipment company into something much more compelling. Along with its iconic green-and-yellow tractors, it now provides software that advises farmers on weather conditions, pinpoints exactly when and how to plant, and anticipates maintenance needs. Instead of working to make its machinery ever faster and sturdier, it started with the most urgent problems its customers faced and worked backward from there. As a result, Deere was able to expand its view of its mission. Instead of aspiring to be the world's best tractor maker, it now aspires to be the best at helping farmers maximize productivity.

Ping An highlights how boldness can take many forms. The Chinese financial conglomerate followed an ecosystem approach. Since 2013, Ping An has expanded beyond its core insurance business and accumulated nearly 500 million online users, created 11 new digital platforms across industries, and increased its number of insurance agents to 1.4 million, all of whom use digital tools and apps created by the business.[7]

These examples highlight another characteristic of success: the importance of leading the charge. Our research shows that companies that fail to get out in front on digital will on average see a decline in revenues of 12 percent. Those that can lead from the front with a disruptive strategy (and at least decent execution), on the other hand, will see gains of 16 percent above that depressed level.[8]

Being first, of course, doesn't just mean being the first company to enter a market. It means being first to enter a market *with* the necessary success factors in place, from talent to tech. A fast-follower approach may feel more comfortable, but too often it becomes a rationale for excess caution—and opens up possibilities for faster competitors to steal new and existing markets.

Disruptive strategies are a powerful response to intense digitization within a sector[6]

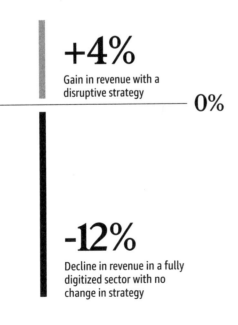

+4%

Gain in revenue with a disruptive strategy

— 0%

-12%

Decline in revenue in a fully digitized sector with no change in strategy

A bold approach is reflected in investment decisions as well. Incumbent companies that are serious about transformation invest triple that of their peers in new technologies, are more likely to acquire digital companies, and are willing to cannibalize their own core.[9] Leading companies are also investing much more in AI: of the most digitized companies, 19 percent say more than one-fifth of their overall digitization spending goes toward AI, while just 8 percent of other respondents say the same.[10]

Prepare for disruption

The need to see the big picture and take bold actions flows from an uncomfortable reality: in the technology age, disruption is just over the horizon . . . or even closer. It's notoriously difficult for companies with a long history of success to see catastrophe looming. Often they have been lulled into a belief that the protective moat around their business is a lot wider and deeper than it actually is.

There are ways, however, of guarding against an attack. Disruptions are not like earthquakes or hurricanes, or other acts of god. They don't just appear out of nowhere. They are the result of forces that can be monitored. So dedicating yourself to focusing on and tracking external activities is a critical success factor. Companies that understand the forces at play and the implications for their own sectors can move themselves from the category of potential "disruptee" to future disruptor.

Essentially, digital opens dramatic new ways to rapidly address market inefficiencies. Even loyal customers who have put up with buying more than they need, waiting longer than they want, or paying more than they should will leave in a heartbeat if a company with a better business model credibly enters the market.

Andy Grove, a Silicon Valley pioneer and former head of Intel, had a pithy phrase for dealing with these business vulnerabilities: "Only the paranoid survive." The title of his 1988 book of the same name highlighted the need to adapt quickly when circumstances change. His key point was that you need to be diligent in looking for threats (or opportunities) so you have the time to adapt.

Staying current on the news and attending industry and other functions are good starts. But you also need to adopt more of a venture-capital (VC) mind-set to analyze changes in customer behavior and follow funding rounds of promising start-ups. This market intelligence initiative should be

Companies that drive more value from analytics than their peers invest more and smarter[11]

13x

More likely to spend more of their IT budget on analytics

2.5x

More likely to plan to spend more on analytics

less about defending your current business and much more about finding opportunities to change the supply-demand dynamic of your market by building a better business model. To maintain a healthy level of paranoia, companies need a person or team dedicated to monitoring and measuring disruptive threats and opportunities in the marketplace.

Truly paranoid companies are also eager to soak up new information and meet with outside experts, analysts, advisors—anyone who can expose them to new points of view. In our experience, arrogance and an unwillingness to listen to others is an early indicator of a company ready to head off the rails.

Be flexible

One of the biggest factors differentiating top digital performers is how adaptable they are in setting, executing, and adjusting their strategies. A digital organization is in a constant state of flux, forever learning and adapting in response to changes in the market, technology, and customer preferences. Leaders at these organizations are continuously scanning the horizon for trends and opportunities, evaluating their worth and assessing their own ability to go after them. To do so, they must constantly toggle between going fast to execute and pulling back to scan the horizon and assess the situation.

How do companies pull this off? Recent McKinsey research[13] analyzed the frequency with which companies follow operational practices of digital strategy. With the exception of mergers and acquisitions (M&A)—which typically require a much longer time frame than the other activities, often due to regulatory reasons—respondents in the top revenue and earnings before interest and taxes (EBIT) decile say their companies carry out each more frequently than their peers.[14]

This kind of rapid iteration happens primarily at two levels and two speeds. At the C-suite or program level, it looks a lot like a dynamic portfolio reallocation exercise. One international retailer revisits its strategic operating plan each quarter. Senior decision-makers review the progress of strategic initiatives. At these meetings, the team reviews results, assesses what was learned, and revisits whether a significant business opportunity still exists, and if so, whether course corrections, resources, and additional investments are needed to drive it forward. If progress isn't clear, the group may elect to stop the initiative.

New analytic techniques can power disruptive new models across sectors[12]

Hyperscale, real-time matching
Insurance
Human capital/talent
Transportation and logistics

Radical personalization
Retail
Media
Education

Massive data integration capabilities
Banking
Public sector
Human capital/talent

Data-driven discovery
Life sciences and pharmaceuticals
Material sciences
Technology

Enhanced decision-making
Smart cities
Health care
Human capital/talent

At the project level where individual initiatives are taking place, strategic check-ins happen much more often, sometimes daily. The strategy is organic, and built to evolve based on continuous market validation. Teams rapidly iterate on minimum viable products (MVPs). As one executive at a large telecom company said, in recalling their transformation program, "We only anticipated about 40 percent of the issues. You just can't plan your way through a transformation."

One of those unforeseen issues was a security flaw that allowed hackers to use stolen credit cards to order multiple new phones. The team had to trace the source of the fraud, which turned out to stem mostly from issues in the supply chain, and fix the problem. In the process, they discovered that high-value customers who had a successful fraud resolution experience spent two times more than other customers. So the team shifted resources to develop a state-of-the-art fraud resolution program.

Learning is a hallmark of the digital enterprise in every dimension. Strategy is no exception.

■

Food for thought

A deliberate and diligent approach to identifying where the value is and will be is one of the fastest ways to accelerate a digital transformation.

Value resides in the many opportunities for improvement in your current operations as well as big, bold new initiatives.

Companies often miss significant sources of value in optimizing current businesses and processes because they have limited expertise in understanding what's possible with digital.

Once they have identified opportunities, the best performing businesses move swiftly and boldly, bringing all necessary resources to bear in their effort to create value.

Leaders with a healthy dose of paranoia are constantly on the lookout for new opportunities and move quickly once they find them.

Effective strategy is reflected in how often it's revisited and how quickly it's executed.

Are you a target for disruption?[15]
If the answer to any of these questions is "yes", you may be open to disruption.

Are your customers subject to intermediaries and their associated fees?

Do your customers face long lead times to complete transactions or to receive products?

Are your margins higher than in other industries?

Is there an opportunity to unbundle products and services?

Is the user experience you provide below the level of the best global practices?

Is supplier information less than fully transparent to customers?

Are you confident that you have an accurate picture of how your organization is really doing?

Multiple factors, from internal naval-gazing to poor data and biases, could prevent you from understanding what's really going on in your business, or what could be going on, if you changed it.

How can you get to where you're going if you don't know where you already are? That might sound like a question a self-help guru would ask, but it's actually a crucial one for companies to answer when you start or reboot a digital transformation. The starting point for any change is self-knowledge. You need to understand your current strengths and weaknesses before you can figure out what you need to do to improve.

Running a diagnostic or self-assessment is the natural answer, but the truth is, getting a good picture of a company's current performance is surprisingly difficult for most businesses. Leaders face formidable and often-hidden barriers, from poor access to reliable data, to conscious and unconscious bias that disguises their company's true performance. This leads to uninformed talk and assumptions, but not a fact-based and clear sense of how the company is actually doing or where it could be heading.

You don't have to be great at everything

We've noticed two extremes as companies grapple with what to measure to understand their performance and health: the first is a natural temptation to "measure everything" to get a comprehensive view of the company. This leads to wasted effort. The second is a tendency to put too much emphasis on a narrow set of indicators such as technology, for example, while down-playing the importance of culture and capabilities.

It's most useful to focus on understanding how the company is doing in those areas that create value. McKinsey's Digital Quotient® analysis found that there are 18 management practices across four areas—strategy, organization, culture, and capabilities—that have the greatest impact on digital performance. Understanding how you stack up in these areas is a good place to start when trying to figure out what's holding back your organization. Dig into how your various business units and teams make decisions in these areas. Are they consistent? Do they make sense? Are they aligned with the larger organizational goals?

Get the data that matters

Companies generate a lot of data. The volume of data generated globally increased by a factor of seven from 2012 to 2016.[17] But on average, US retailers, for example, capture only 30–40 percent of the value of their data. For manufacturers, it's only 20–30 percent.[18] This helps explain the inability of businesses to tame their data to develop a clear view of how they're performing.

Advances in analytics and data networking help address this problem by making it possible to measure data faster and at a more granular level than even a few years ago. Even without adding any new capabilities, most companies should be able to get exact numbers on important metrics, such as the cost of fulfillment on an hourly basis. They should know up to the minute where they stand on hiring and training. Same thing for channel, marketing mix, and ROI performance. Coaxing meaning from your data requires some heavy lifting, technologically speaking. Broadly, it requires setting common standards (e.g., service level agreements), designing principles (e.g., simplifying the data environment), and a governance model to manage and structure the data itself. And then you need a system to integrate the data sources.

Data management is obviously a massive task, so it's important to be clear about what the output should be or else you'll spend years working on data that doesn't actually help with decisions. Start by selecting and enhancing "golden source" data repositories (i.e., data that provides the most useful insights). That data then feeds a continuously updated dashboard that provides hourly—rather than daily or weekly—updates that the entire leadership team can access. The dashboard should be set up to automatically alert you to numbers that exceed the tolerances or exceptions you set. The goal is to provide up-to-the-minute insights about your operations that allow you to convert data into faster and better decision-making.

Time to up your Digital Quotient (DQ)[16]

A high DQ score, measured across four outcomes, correlates with stronger digital and financial performance.

1

Strategy

Bold, long-term orientation

Linked to business strategy

Centered on customer needs

2

Culture

Higher tolerance for risk

Greater speed and agility

Test-and-learn approach

International collaboration

External orientation

3

Organization

New roles and responsibilities

Greater focus on talent and leadership

Well thought out governance/KPIs

Digital investment

4

Capabilities

Connectivity

Content creation

Customer experience

Data-driven decision-making

Automation

IT architecture

Just as important as getting the data is agreeing on it. We've seen plenty of situations where one executive won't agree with another because they're each relying on a different set of data. Without a single source of truth and a discipline around using common measures, biases run rampant.

Get past the biases

Along with the lack of top-notch data and insights, there's another, more subtle obstacle that often prevents companies from achieving the level of self-awareness they need.

We're talking about a kind of cultural blindness that prevents some companies from recognizing what the data is telling them. It often results from bias, which comes in many different forms. The Nobel Prize–winning behavioral economist Daniel Kahneman has identified an array of unconscious biases that lead to flawed decision-making. The tendency to confuse historic structural advantages—or even luck—for skill, which can lead you to overestimate your own abilities, is one example.

Companies seem particularly prone to the unconscious or not-so-unconscious bias toward good news—and a propensity for rewarding the people who deliver it. If managers fear a ding to their annual performance review or a cutback in resources, they may be looking for data cuts that tell a positive story—even as the overall picture deteriorates. In this kind of culture, no one is rewarded for digging into numbers that don't promote the accepted view that all is well. And the truth is, almost any operation can look like a success if you just cut the data in the right way.

Closely related to this is the bias that causes us to seek out and overvalue data that supports our existing beliefs. Psychologists have long noted this tendency to unconsciously bolster the conclusion we've already drawn—and the ways in which it can distort decision-making.

The CEO of a UK manufacturer saw a variation of this issue when he suspected several of his leaders were unreliable as sources of information. To overcome any implicit bias, he turned to an AI team to create and train algorithms on a wide variety of data sources (e.g., project life-cycle management, fine-grained design and manufacturing documents, financial and HR data).

The team examined the number of emails sent after meetings or to other departments, the use of enterprise chat groups and length of chats, and texting volume, among other things, and discovered a problem. The IT and design departments were barely collaborating at all. The team was also able to provide clear evidence that poor collaboration slowed time to market and increased costs.[19]

Some CEOs find their own ways to learn what's happening deep in their organizations. Indra Nooyi, former CEO of PepsiCo, made a point of visiting grocery stores every week, just to see what her products looked like on the shelves. If she didn't like what she saw, she would whip out her cell phone and send photos—with notes—to the design and marketing teams responsible.

Jaap Postma, CEO of Nuuday and member of the Executive Committee of TDC, the Danish telecom, drove a successful agile transformation of digital services. He made a point of visiting the digital squads working on new initiatives. He relied on visual work tools designed for a customer-focused, agile delivery, which made it much easier for him to interact with the teams and give feedback.

F. D. Wilder
Former Senior Vice
President, Global Market
Strategy & Innovation
Procter & Gamble

Facing up to reality

"To get a realistic view of where we stood, we've adopted a 'no mercy, no malice' mantra. Translation: There's no time for posturing; just tell it to me straight! This started about five years ago, when e-commerce was only 2 percent of our business, yet digital was affecting over 50 percent of our total sales.

Along with other key leaders and experts, I was tasked to lead our e-business growth strategy and raise our digital IQ—recognizing that digital transformation is a 'team sport.' It was immediately apparent we could benefit from an outside point of view to benchmark our performance versus our best competitors. That led us to the NYU Stern School of Business, where a professor had developed an algorithm to calculate the digital IQ of brands correlated to value creation.

We partnered with the team to calculate the digital IQ scores of our brands and build our digital capabilities. When the program started to yield results, the CEO (A. G. Lafley at that time) asked us to present what we were doing and learning at our annual top-management meeting. We started with a digital IQ test to assess base-level understanding. More than 50 percent of the group did not pass—illuminating the case for change and galvanizing our business leaders to commit to meaningful digital transformation."

■

Food for thought

Many companies have a surprisingly flawed understanding of their own current strengths and weaknesses—making it difficult to create a strategy for transformation.

Getting more out of the data you have through better data management can help you get a handle on where you stand.

Align on a "single source of truth" for your data, to speed up and improve decision-making.

Even with better data, internal biases could be preventing you from getting a more accurate picture of your performance.

See for yourself what's happening in your business.

Will your strategy work in the real world?

Great strategies and promising experiments often stumble due to lack of clarity on implementation, or thoughtful planning for how to sustain and scale initial impact.

Strategies for building a digital business that learns, adapts, and captures big gains may look great on the drawing board. But translating those strategies into actual value is another thing altogether.

We won't go into all the many tasks that are necessary here, but we will highlight two of the most consistent issues we see that stymie transformations:

Understand 'last-mile' complexity

Modern businesses are complex and deeply interconnected organizations. While a new digital initiative might promise huge value, you won't see much of it if you don't take into account all the people and systems that have to make it happen. This is the well-known but often poorly understood "last-mile challenge," that is, the often-complex interdependencies at the edge of the organization that can lead to ineffective decision-making and slow down change.

A single product designed to improve customer experience in buying a new banking service, for example, might require training people in R&D, procurement, operations, marketing, sales, customer service, and other areas to work in different ways to support the new product.

Incumbents routinely underestimate the effort required, leading to squandered value and low adoption rates of technologies that otherwise could

"Everyone has a plan 'til they get punched in the mouth."[20]

Mike Tyson

have a large impact on the business. Only 6 percent of frontline workers embed AI into formal decision-making and execution processes, for example, while only 16 percent of employees trust AI-generated insights, according to a McKinsey survey on AI adoption.[21]

Here's what the last-mile challenge looks like in practice for a global mining company that was trying to improve productivity. One strand of that effort was to use analytics and move to predictive maintenance to reduce costs and decrease downtime. To make sure it captured the value of shifting to a maintenance schedule based on need rather than set intervals, the company also had to shift the work routines of its maintenance-related experts. The reliability experts learned to triage predicted maintenance events, the planning team created a new scheduling procedure to avoid excess downtime, and the inventory management team found new ways to restock to ensure the right parts were on hand when equipment was brought in.[22]

When it comes to analytics, winning companies spend a disproportionate amount of their energies and resources trying to break through the last-mile challenge. Nearly 90 percent of the best performers devote more than half of their analytics budgets to this effort, versus only 23 percent of all other organizations.[23] In practice, this means making analytics user-friendly and tailored to a given person or team of people so they can make better decisions. And it requires embedding analytics into existing processes and tools, which are familiar to the end user. A major retailer saw a significant increase in sales by delivering demographic data on customers to store managers on a daily basis and empowering them to act on the insights.

To help overcome last-mile problems, the best companies build training and adoption explicitly into their rollouts.

90%

Proportion of winning companies that devote more than half their analytics budgets to solving last-mile challenges.

Make it concrete

At the end of the movie *The Candidate*, a politician (played by Robert Redford) who has just won the race for the US Senate turns to his campaign manager amid the celebrations and asks, "What do we do now?" That's a familiar question for people faced with translating lofty digital plans and aspirations into action.

McKinsey analysis has found that one of the most important moves in turning a strategy into a reality is galvanizing action to take the first step. Leaders need to identify the actions necessary to get started. This can be, for example, tackling staffing to put the best people on a few key initiatives. Or providing teams with clear, proximate goals of what can be achieved and verified over the first three to six months. It's important to bear in mind that at this stage, tracking actions taken is more meaningful than tracking results delivered. Focusing too much on the latter will strangle progress.

Take AI and analytics programs. Best practice is to identify three to five concrete use cases that are feasible and generate value. With each successful use case completed, the company builds confidence and skills to make further progress. That lesson is clear when getting value from the Internet of Things (IoT) as well. We have found that the greatest bottom-line value from IoT comes from trying multiple use cases, each grounded on a clear business case tied to the strategy, and executing them with discipline. In fact, we've found that implementing more use cases correlates with better financial impact.[24]

Creating a roadmap to help show the way forward has an important role to play as well in translating strategy into action. While this might seem like a vestige of the old days, the very complexity of a transformation—along with the need to be flexible enough to adapt as you learn—makes a roadmap crucial. This is not a waterfall planning activity. But it's an important discipline for looking ahead and spotting dependencies, constraints, and issues as well as thinking through which initiatives to focus on. In this way, developing roadmaps helps companies overcome pilot paralysis by making an overwhelming and chaotic challenge manageable and affordable.

One electronics company, for example, that was transforming its manufacturing operations took the time to define more than 100 applications it wanted. Based on the maturity of the underlying technologies each would need and each initiative's potential ROI, the company narrowed the list to 30 and further refined it to three waves of 10 each that it would roll out over two years.[25] This made it easier to assign people and resources, and then manage them.

Alain Bejjani, the CEO of conglomerate Majid Al Futtaim, has built flexibility and accountability into making sure his vision for the company translates the organization's strategy into action. Each month, he meets with his business unit (BU) leaders to track performance and develop strategies, but also to understand what concrete initiatives they're delivering to implement the company's vision. The BU leaders take that same approach with their own senior managers, who in turn both challenge and strategize with their respective managers around how they are driving toward the company's vision. This cascading approach gives teams the flexibility to implement programs they think will be most effective in delivering on the vision while also building accountability into the process.

To understand how well the vision is being implemented at the edge of the organization, Bejjani also hosts Top Talent lunches twice a month with employees across the businesses at all levels of seniority. These lunches (#TalentLunchSeries) allow him to get a better sense of how well people understand the company's vision and to generate ideas to improve the organization's customer-first transformation. As Bejjani posted on his Instagram feed: "Ensuring we create time to listen to voices from across our organization is critical to effective leadership."

Creating a roadmap is a program-level activity, tied to your vision and your long-term goals for the transformation. For this reason, the program-level roadmap is fairly stable, though by no means is it set in stone.

■

Food for thought

To translate strategy into value, you need to make sure the organization has thought through how the change happens on the ground.

Roadmapping is not a "waterfall" exercise but instead provides stability to the transformation by helping to prioritize initiatives and anticipating both needs and roadblocks.

Focus on the first steps people need to take. It helps to jump-start and guide initial activities.

A key element of a good roadmap is identifying three to five use cases that are feasible, generate value, and can be accomplished in the first year.

Once you know the path, you need to make sure that everyone in the organization, down to the front line, understands the overall steps and their own specific roles.

The program-level roadmap should be aligned to the company's strategy and vision, and so shouldn't change significantly.

Are you clear about which transformation model is best for your company?

4

There are several different ways to launch, scale, and sustain digital initiatives. The best companies are purposeful about picking the right mix.

Before a company throws itself into a transformation, it has to make some big and difficult decisions: Buy or build? Start small or go big? Overhaul the existing business or place bets on something new? Essentially, this is about choosing a transformation model that makes sense for your company's situation. Making the right decision requires thoughtful deliberation about where to start and what your aspiration is for your brand, talent, and market position.

That deliberation should include a careful assessment of your industry and your company's position within the industry, especially in regard to disruption (for more on this, please read the chapter "Are you confident that you have an accurate picture of how your organization is really doing?"). In some industries, the disruptions are existential, requiring radical action. In other cases, the threat is farther off on the horizon, providing companies with more flexibility in choosing how to respond. In yet other cases, where margins are low and barriers high, focused improvements can be the best choice.

As you might expect, there is no one model for change. In fact, the most successful companies take advantage of multiple models. Our research shows that those incumbents making big digital moves to reinvent their core business model *and* compete digitally in new markets are significantly outperforming their peers.[26] Even as you determine the right mix for your business situation, it's important to remember that while one model should be the primary focus, the mix is likely to evolve over time as both your organization itself and the marketplace change. There are four main models to consider.

Transform the core

This is the full monty of transformations. It involves a fundamental rebuilding of the company's core skills, technology, organization, and processes. Change happens at scale across multiple parts of the business at the same time.

One approach to driving this change is to map out all your customer journeys—those sets of activities your customers undertake to complete a specific goal—and to transform one journey at a time (working up to doing more in parallel). Since each journey touches many parts of the business—operations, marketing, service support, sales, IT—this approach serves as an organizing principle for making changes to core systems that support the customer.

Danish telecom company TDC took this approach, launching 12 agile teams—cross-functional "squads" consisting of product owners, commercial specialists, frontline experts, customer-experience designers, architects, and developers. These squads were accountable for specific customer journeys as they embarked on rapid test-and-learn programs. TDC also moved its entire B2C IT in-house. Previously, it had assigned three-quarters of the work to vendors. Creative approaches to finding and hiring talent enabled a massive shift where three-quarters of IT talent was brought in-house within 18 months. The changes quickly had impact. Eighty percent of TDC's customers gave its onboarding experience five stars. Call volume, one of TDC's biggest costs, fell by more than 40 percent.

We are also increasingly seeing companies take a more radical variation of this approach where they make big changes all at once rather than more incrementally. This approach to a core transformation requires a greater effort, but results can happen within a year as opposed to as long as five years through the more staged and incremental approach. Dutch bank ING undertook this "big bang" approach to become agile so they could be more responsive to customers and get improvements in the field faster. The company focused on the headquarters, to show what was possible. Within nine months, all 3,500 workers at ING's headquarters were working in agile tribes and squads, many of them in new roles.

When does it make sense to consider this model?

- There is a strong top leader who is willing to devote 100 percent of his or her time to drive the change.

- The C-suite is explicitly aligned on the need for significant transformation.

- There is already a strong foundation of capable people, even if they need training to develop digital skills.

- The existing brand is strong, and an asset in hiring.

- The core business is facing existential threats and loss of revenue from disruptors.

- Leadership is willing to make a major budget commitment over several years.

- The culture is open to innovation.

Pitfalls

- Because a full-scale core transformation can be hard to complete, leadership support can fade.

- If the IT architecture cannot separate slow back-end processes from responsive front-end ones, it will be difficult to create good applications quickly.

- Flipping the switch can be scary, requiring companies to move at a pace that can feel almost chaotic.

2

Start
or
buy
a new
business

In this model, the company either builds or acquires a new business. While admittedly there is a significant difference between building or acquiring a business, each has the advantage of providing the new venture with the flexibility to attract and retain talent and to forge its own culture and identity. If it's homegrown, it can develop completely new processes and ways of working to perform like a digital native. Often a new digital business can be built from scratch in much less time (6–12 months) than it takes to upgrade legacy processes.

In some cases, when the threat of disruption is imminent, for example, it may make more sense to quickly acquire digital properties, as German publishing company Axel Springer has done. Since 2011, it has purchased 16 digital properties, allowing it to transform into Europe's largest digital publisher.[27] In fact, recent McKinsey analysis showed that winning companies report spending more than twice as much on M&A, as a share of annual revenue, as their counterparts.

A variation of this model is to invest in external start-ups and digital businesses, which can provide companies with access to talent and capabilities, as well as cash flow. Since 2013, Axel Springer has also been active on this front, making more than 90 investments in early-stage businesses.[28]

A Brazilian financial leader, Caixa Seguradora, took another path by building Youse, a completely independent direct-to-consumer (DTC) digital insurance business, because its research showed the first mover won 30 percent of market share and there was no other DTC insurer. Youse released a series of minimum viable products, learning and adjusting along the way. After three years of massive growth, the business generated positive returns.

When does it make sense to consider this model?

- Existing internal talent lacks experience creating new products and services quickly.

- Existing brand is a detriment to hiring digital stars.

- Existing company culture is not capable of nurturing a digital business.

- Leadership is not ready to make the commitment necessary for a complete digital transformation.

- The incumbent has valuable assets it can use with the new business (e.g., proprietary data, customer base, market position).

- Competitive threats make speed crucial in terms of sustaining and scaling the change.

- Leadership accepts the possibility that the new venture will cannibalize existing business.

- The business has a successful track record of acquiring and integrating companies.

Pitfalls

- Management is too focused on the incumbent business and doesn't provide the new business with sufficient support.

- A culture of digital "haves" and "have-nots" can grow if there is significant compensation and career-path disparity.

Transform from the edge

The basic idea here is to nurture a new digital capability that is protected from the company while still taking advantage of the organization's core competencies and existing resources. For a pharma company, that could be its R&D capability. For an auto company, it could be its factory network. Often, this "edge" approach comes to life through a digital factory or center of excellence, a hub for coders and other technology specialists who develop, prototype, and launch applications. These are then fed back into the core company and scaled. The factory serves as a model for the rest of the business by demonstrating new ways of working. The best digital factories can put a new product or customer experience into production in as little as 10 weeks and scale it across the business in 8 to 12 months.[29]

One European bank dedicated several floors at its headquarters to its digital factory, complete with new team work spaces that made collaboration easy and an HR "war room" to innovate how to hire top talent (e.g., hosting tech events and assiduously tracking recruiting performance).

Each floor of the factory focused on a separate digital project to create a reusable bit of technology, such as customer identification and verification or e-signatures. To make sure that the new products and solutions developed by the factory were adopted, business leaders and IT were involved from the beginning. IT knew what was coming down the digital-factory line so it could set up and configure systems to support the new journeys and processes. A combination of on-the-job training and incentives was crucial in driving adoption.

When does it make sense to consider this model?

- There is a strong internal advocate at the business unit level (or higher).

- There is a broad commitment to digital transformation but not yet to the level of a core transformation.

- There is significant value potential through digitalization of existing business lines.

- The existing brand has significant value and is continuing to grow.

- There is a distinct digital/analytics need at the business unit level, though not necessarily across the entire business.

- Transforming the core is too complex to undertake wholesale.

- Existing talent and technology cannot support a transformation of the core.

- There is no immediate threat of wholesale disruption.

Pitfalls

- The digital factory isn't sufficiently protected and is slowly "smothered" by process and culture of the incumbent.

- Adoption and integration processes are not in place to ensure new products developed by the digital factory are actually used.

- A divisive culture of digital "haves" and "have-nots" can grow if there is significant compensation and career-path disparity.

- Leadership does not commit to an active rotation program to expose employees to new ways of working in the digital factory.

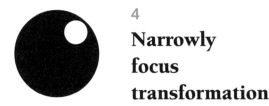

Narrowly focus transformation

In a limited transformation, companies look for a particular lever where digital can increase value. It may be a function, like marketing or logistics, or even a product line or region. Companies using this model look for particular opportunities where they can make gains without affecting the larger organization and culture.

This model makes sense for companies in industries that are simply more resistant to digitalization. The industry may be based more on personal relationships, artisanal, or may have more complex logistics that offer only limited opportunities for automation. Luxury and grocery retailing offer good examples of industries that have been relatively slow to change. Since fresh food, for instance, must be shipped, displayed, sold, and consumed in a short period of time, logistics are difficult. But with its low margins, even a partial transformation that yields a small percentage gain could have a dramatic effect on profitability, which some companies are recognizing, leading to accelerating change in that industry.

Similarly, a global chemicals distributor felt protected by its close customer relationships for many years. But when it realized it was getting squeezed by new competitors that were starting to go straight to customers at a lower cost to serve and price, the distributor knew it needed to improve salesforce productivity. So it developed a website and an app that were customized to various users.

Customers had a version that was unique to them, with product recommendations tailored to their needs (e.g., a restaurant owner would see grease-removal options) and a simple reordering function. The salespeople had an app that allowed them to customize 200 core products across thousands of permutations in real time based on a client's needs. This approach

allowed the company to quickly cut operating expenses by 2 percent, and increase total revenue per existing customer by 4 percent. This also freed up more time for salespeople to win new business.

When does it make sense to consider this model?

- Industry characteristics (e.g., need for personal interactions) make digitalization less attractive.

- Specific functions can be singled out for digitalization without disrupting the overall operations and culture.

- The threat of disruption is low.

- Business relies on complex logistics or significant "brick-and-mortar" overhead.

- Existing customer satisfaction levels are high.

Pitfalls

- Lack of a profile in the digital world will make talent acquisition and retention difficult.

- A lack of in-house talent will require outside partners—and the expertise to manage those partners.

- The digital function must learn to coexist within a larger nondigital culture.

Do you know what great looks like?

5

Seeing is believing, whether that's understanding how the best digital companies perform or experiencing firsthand just how fast "fast companies" can really be.

While companies understand they need to "get better" or "become more digital," it is often hard to know what that means in practice. Many business leaders simply don't know what they don't know. In this vacuum, leaders will tend to set their aspirations too low or focus on the wrong elements of a transformation. Understanding what the best companies are doing, and how they're doing it, can dramatically shift what leaders think is possible.

Go and see

In the second half of the 19th century, Japan found itself secluded and vulnerable. To avoid falling victim to the colonial powers as many of his neighbors had, the Emperor Meiji realized Japan needed a full-scale transformation. One of the first moves the new emperor made was to send a delegation of more than 100 representatives to tour the United States and Europe to learn as much as possible about Western societies. After two years, armed with new knowledge and a new resolve, the delegation returned to Japan and began a modernization program that would transform the country from a closed, medieval society to a modern—and independent—power.

That's an important lesson for today's leaders. The best way to understand what's happening is often just to get outside of your own four walls to see agile companies in action. This is the time to work your networks. Engage the most digitally savvy members of your board to help you identify and get inside those organizations. Tap former executives, experts, advisors, professional organizations, consultants—anyone who can help you gain entrée. Even customers are a possibility.

The leaders and board of Spark, a New Zealand telecom company, visited 12 companies on three continents as they considered a transformation, to properly understand what agile looked like in action and the magnitude of change required. One CEO told us that even though he'd heard multiple explanations of how agile worked, he only understood it after visiting a retail company and seeing agile teams at work.

What we've found most effective is "active observation"—not just looking at how people are working, but asking questions about what they're doing and why. That can include asking what roles people have in an agile team, how they track progress, and what helps them do their jobs effectively. It should include asking what customers they're focusing on and why, what the product or service a team is working on is supposed to do, and what they've learned from experiments so far. This spirit of inquiry is fundamental to understanding what works and what doesn't.

How do you know if you're really seeing digital in action?

When visiting another company, look for these markers:

Team spaces have whiteboards for collaboration and public dashboards that show what every team member is working on.

Employees are engaged. They're often in animated conversation solving a problem.

Team members are happy to chat and can talk easily about the digital technologies they're using.

The office layout is open and changeable, with lots of homey, casual meeting spaces and quirky touches. Snacks and drinks are readily available.

The layout is team-friendly. Think shared tables for working and larger spaces for all-hands meetings.

What fast looks like

Just because a digital transformation is a long-term effort that requires endurance and commitment doesn't mean you can't make swift, material gains. In fact, if that's not happening, something's wrong.

Low expectations permeate many incumbent businesses, where traditional ways of doing things are the default operating mode. When the CDO of a large US retailer said he wanted to launch a new business, the CIO said it would take at least 500 people four years, and cost $100 million. That was a good faith estimate based on how IT worked. But the CDO understood digital and knew he could move much more quickly. So instead he chose to hire a new team and move it to a new location so it could work independently. Within five months, the business was generating incremental revenues of $150 million per month, the equivalent of nearly $2 billion annualized.

Understanding what is possible with digital means that quick wins can be even quicker—and bigger—than imagined. In many cases, in fact, significant wins are achievable in just days or even hours, and those gains can be a powerful way to shift expectations of what it means to move quickly. They prove the art of the possible, urging the transformation forward and reinforcing cultural change.

Examples of quick wins include using low-cost tools to expand a keyword list from hundreds to thousands to improve search-engine marketing in a matter of hours, optimizing websites for all devices, and improving load times for digital assets (for each second your site or app is slower than what is perceived to be acceptable, click or buy conversions can fall by up to 40 percent). On the surface, these changes seem trivial, so many companies overlook them. But when companies do make these kinds of changes, it's surprising how much they can move the needle.

One large retail company made huge gains in a single day by attending to exactly these changes. The starting point was a website that took 16 seconds to load, kept crashing (uptime was just 89 percent), and was not compatible with mobile devices. Not only was the customer experience dreadful, the company was also paying four times more than it should have for search terms because its site was not mobile-responsive.

To improve matters, the company expanded the number of keywords that would bring potential customers to the site with the help of simple-to-use software. This took two hours.

In parallel, it completed an outside-in user experience review, identifying small tweaks that it implemented immediately as well as larger, longer-term improvements that would boost conversion rates and reduce the bounce rate. In a single day, site traffic increased by 5 percent and marketing spend dropped more than 3 percent. At the end of one week, traffic from digital marketing increased 15 percent while conversion rates rose 31 percent, even as spending dropped 16 percent. At the same time, daily website errors dropped from nearly 6,100 to under 4,800. The sum of all this? Over 30 percent improvement in run rate revenue.

Four months on, the numbers were better still:

- Traffic up 125 percent
- Marketing spend down 47 percent
- Conversion rate up 130 percent
- Website load time down to 4.1 seconds
- Fewer than 700 daily system errors

We have seen time and again how rapid cycles of impact energize teams, which get hooked on the rush of satisfaction and accomplishment. And when people elsewhere in the organization see how much can be accomplished in such a short period, they want some of it for themselves and so

What fast looks like

By using technology and agile practices to speed processes, companies can move much faster.

	Normal	Fast
Product launch	6 months	2 weeks
New hires, application to offer	6 months	3 weeks
Marketing campaign	1 per month	24 per day
Code release	1 every 6 months	1 per day
Consumer product concept tests	1 in 6 months	3 in 14 weeks

start competing. This spreading urge to get quick results speeds the organization's learning metabolism. Ideas that were once debated for months before anyone dared to give them a try can now quickly be piloted. And as value is unlocked, pride builds in the organization.

■

Food for thought

Visit the best digital companies to understand what great looks like in action.

Don't wait weeks or months to get results. Significant improvements can happen in days or even hours.

Small and seemingly trivial changes can have massive impact.

Quick wins are powerful drivers of cultural change, energizing teams that get hooked on the rush of satisfaction and accomplishment.

CAPABILITIES

Have you made it safe to fail?

6

Learning and failing go hand in hand, but unless people feel safe, they won't take chances.

When Thomas Edison was asked if he regretted all his failed tests on light bulbs, he famously responded, "I have not failed. I've just found 10,000 ways that won't work." Most people find it hard to be quite so sanguine as Mr. Edison about failure. It goes against human nature.

Ed Catmull, the co-founder of Pixar, explains the psychology: "One of the things about failure is that it's asymmetrical with respect to time. When you look back and see failure, you say, 'It made me what I am!' But looking forward, you think, 'I don't know what is going to happen, and I don't want to fail.' The difficulty is that when you're running an experiment, it's forward-looking. We have to try extra hard to make it safe to fail."[30]

Making it safe to fail is crucial because learning happens through experimentation, and experimentation often results in failure. Recent McKinsey research shows, in fact, that respondents at successful organizations are more than twice as likely as their peers elsewhere to strongly agree that employees are rewarded for taking risks of an appropriate level.[31] So a willingness to fail has to be embedded in a company's culture. Many companies have gotten good at saying that it's safe to fail, but for most people that's not enough. Human nature being what it is, risk aversion (even fear) will rule people's actions if they don't actually believe it's safe to fail.

At one telecom company, for example, a team working with an outside vendor passed what it felt was a tricky decision to its manager, who referred it all the way to the CEO's desk. The CEO then called the CEO of the vendor to try to resolve the issue. This game of "pass the buck" happened four times as lower-level teams and managers were unwilling to make decisions, fearful they might be the wrong ones.

Companies have to put in place various "safety nets" to allow a culture of experimentation to take hold. Here are a few ways we've seen companies successfully combat this kind of fear:

Tech designed to make it safe to try

Technology can minimize the consequences of failing, which can often inhibit people from trying something new. Advances in tech have, in fact, made failure cheap, fast, and reversible. Automated software testing, for example, means code failures can be spotted in seconds, allowing fixes to be made without putting significant parts of the business at risk. The most sophisticated companies can even roll back website changes to fix issues with a single system command. Performance tests can measure the system under load or stress, and security tests measure its resilience against malicious attacks.

One international consumer-goods company migrated its software to the cloud so it could give developers self-service access to production-like environments for testing and delegate the execution of thousands of automated tests to "virtual servers" that take seconds to run.

Pharma companies, meanwhile, are turning to advanced analytics and machine learning to scale the number of tests on new drugs and the quality of the results, reducing the chances of costly wrong turns and speeding drug development. Some high-volume testing (for microbial detection and water sterility, for example) can be performed online rather than in physical labs, through automation. Moving to instantaneous microbial detection for environmental monitoring can reduce overall lab lead time by 40–75 percent.[33]

"Failure" leadership

Like so many things in a digital transformation, change starts at the top. You won't make much progress encouraging people to take risks if the head of the business doesn't show it's really safe to do so. Sam Yagan, ShopRunner CEO, for example, has asked executives in their reviews to describe recent failures. If the failures hadn't cost the company money, the executives didn't get their bonuses.[34]

> "You need to constantly talk about executive failures, even CEO failures. When I was CEO at Match, we acquired a company, and I think I overpaid for it by $50 million. I got up in front of everyone and talked about that—and people were able to see that I was still there. So people could say, 'If he made a $50 million mistake, maybe that's not so bad. Maybe I can make a $50,000 mistake.'"[32]

Sam Yagan
SHOPRUNNER CEO AND FORMER
MATCH GROUP CEO

Microsoft's CEO Satya Nadella famously didn't rant following a high-profile PR debacle when Tay, a bot that had been programmed to interact with Twitter users, was taught by some of those users to spew racist, misogynistic, and pornographic text. Besides grounding the bot and expressing regret for the unintended offense, Nadella also emailed the team that developed Tay, eager to make sure it didn't regret taking the risks they took. "You've got to make sure that if you make mistakes, you learn from [them]," Nadella said.[35] The CEO at a leading retailer took a more active approach to protect his employees so they knew they'd be safe. He made sure that the lead on any project got the credit when an experiment succeeded, but took the blame himself when it failed.

Accepting failure is important as well in encouraging fast decision-making, a key capability in digital companies. The mentality is that a bad decision is better than no decision. Company leaders can lend a helping hand here too. The head of one European retail company, for example, mandated that decisions be made within 30 minutes of the start of any meeting. Another CEO wanted teams to make more of their own decisions rather than escalating them higher up in the organization and delaying progress. His solution? Hold escalation meetings at 11:00 on Saturday mornings. Not surprisingly, teams started making more decisions for themselves.

"Most decisions," Amazon's CEO Jeff Bezos wrote in a 2017 letter to shareholders, "should probably be made with somewhere around 70 percent of the information you wish you had. If you wait for 90 percent, in most cases you're probably being slow."[36]

Clear process and information access

There's another culprit that can undermine efforts to create an environment where it's safe to fail: uncertainty. Putting in place guidelines and processes—and clearly communicating them—helps reduce uncertainty, which in turn provides people with greater confidence to act. Ensuring there is clarity over roles and responsibilities, for example, is absolutely crucial to avoid painful, time-wasting uncertainties.

Access to information also has an important effect in reducing uncertainty. Equipping call-center employees with real-time analysis on account profiles, for example, or data on usage and profitability, empowers them to modify offers in real time as they have the information to gauge their decisions. In the retail and hospitality industries, companies give frontline employees information such as purchase history so they have the confidence to

"We aim to make mistakes faster than anyone else."[37]

Daniel Ek
SPOTIFY FOUNDER

resolve customer issues on the spot, without having to escalate it to management.[38]

One oil and gas company automated the evaluation of several business cases so that it had continuous hard data on how the experiments were going, which reduced anxiety among executives about the firm's digital investment decisions. Indeed, the insights gave them confidence to push ahead with more cutting-edge solutions because they knew they could see in near real time what worked, while failures could be detected quickly and do so relatively cheaply.[39]

Google made a conscious effort to destigmatize failure after it discovered that when employees felt they could take risks without being shamed or criticized for failure, they performed better.[40] So it introduced a process for when any incident is recorded, the team asks questions such as "What went well?" and "Where did we get lucky?" to understand how processes could be improved rather than to find fault. Team leads admit their own mistakes and failures and are willing to document them. Teams are discouraged from blaming anyone and reminded that no one will be punished.[41]

Failing is not always acceptable

It's plain wrong when:

The thinking is lazy or flawed. Any risk should be well thought through. At Amazon, most new ideas require a six-page narrative that describes what the product will look like at launch, and a full Q&A to anticipate customer questions.

There are no mechanisms to track progress and adjust. Metrics, clear escalation paths, and governance processes are required.

People don't share or act on what they've learned. If the business doesn't learn from the failure, what's the point?

■

Food for thought

The CEO has the key role in creating an environment where people understand they won't be punished for failing.

A corporate culture that accepts failure encourages fast decision-making.

Reducing uncertainties and providing people with access to good information give employees the confidence to make more of their own decisions.

Automation and analytics have advanced to the point where "failing fast" is a real option for specific cases, especially testing.

Failure is only acceptable if you learn from it and act on what you learned.

Do you know what it takes to scale an agile culture?

7

Customer centricity and collaboration are essential for making agile part of the business culture.

Agility is the heart and soul of a learn-and-adapt culture. It embodies the idea of people trying something out, testing it in the field, making adjustments based on what they have learned, and then testing it again. Over and over, at speed.

Yet while many companies have notched up notable successes in parts of the organization using an agile approach, those successes have been challenging to extend across the organization. Agile teams therefore often remain something of an exotic curiosity, either hidden in the trenches of IT or isolated as a "show horse" initiative. This is an important issue to address since agile teams are 50 percent more likely to outperform other business teams financially.[42]

Companies need to build a stable backbone of support mechanisms—processes, governance, organizational structures, and technologies—if agile ways of working are to spread across the organization. Too often, companies equate agile with project management, and so fail to build these company-wide supports for agile teams.

Many of the organizational changes required for agile to work at scale are well documented. But here are a few additional practices we think are particularly important to get right though are often underappreciated or misunderstood:

Agile budgeting

For agile initiatives to proceed, you need an agile budgeting process—one that guarantees money can be allocated quickly when it's required. It might seem logical that iterative development requires iterative funding, but this concept is hard to put into practice for many traditional businesses. Budgeting remains one of the more conservative functions in an organization, and therefore resistant to change.

How to organize for agile

An example of how roles and teams can work together.

Tribe

Group of squads with shared mission and targets

Fewer than 150 people to foster effective collaboration

Set regular gatherings to share current status and learnings

Squad

Self-organizing group of people that defines its own way of working

Located physically together

Have skills and tools to design, develop, test, and release their deliverables

Responsible for discrete product or service

Led by product owner

Chapter

Cross-functional competence groups (e.g., programmer)

Meet each other regularly to exchange knowledge

Guild

Informal communities across tribes

Gather people with the same interests, for sharing practices and knowledge

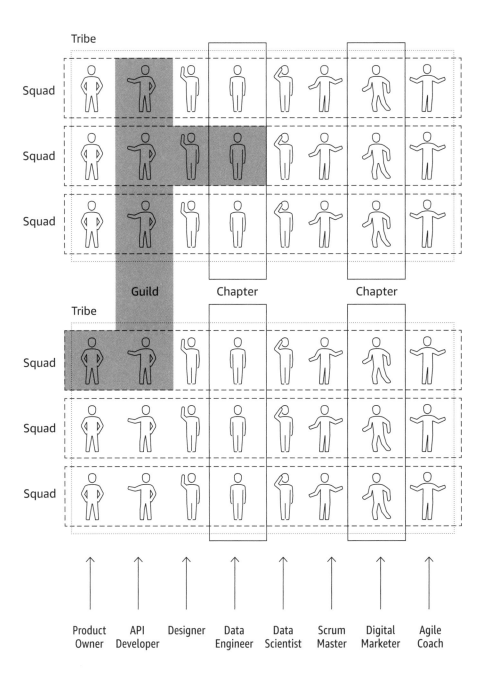

Yet if the process of making funding requests and gaining approval remains mired in layers of bureaucracy, it can kill a transformation—a lesson that one large North American insurance company discovered to its detriment. Its established practice of reviewing funding annually ended up stifling innovation, as it was unable to keep pace with the customer-facing teams that had adopted agile ways of working. These teams were waiting months to find out whether they would get the funding they needed.

Dynamic processes for reallocating budgets should happen throughout the year. Every quarter, the CFO reviews the company's strategic priorities and ensures resources are allocated to organizational units in a way that supports them. She also decides whether units are making progress against strict key performance indicators (KPIs). Funds are then reallocated accordingly. Hereafter, the heads of organizational units are free to decide how the money is spent, reprioritizing or reallocating funds between teams in the unit monthly, weekly, or even daily. In addition, there is a separate pot of money for "venture funding." Anyone with a new idea can pitch for funding every quarter, ensuring new ideas can be tested without delay.

This kind of agile budgeting process ensures not only that the best projects get the funding they need to stay alive or prosper but also that the less promising ones are axed. Although running hundreds of pilots is a great way to cultivate entrepreneurial energy and generate ideas, without a disciplined process for weeding out the bad ones, resources are squandered. So if a project is not in line with strategic objectives, or if KPIs and deadlines have been repeatedly missed, then funds should be withdrawn quickly.

Do not, however, fall into the trap of wanting the entire budget to be allocated in this way. Significant parts of the budget should *not* be agile, such as spend for the risk function. As a rule of thumb, 60 percent of a company's budget should be allocated in the usual way, 30 percent through an agile budgeting process, and 10 percent reserved for venture funding.

Learning to be agile

As Miguel Peña, vice chairman at Naranja, a financial institution in Argentina, said: "Moving people from the traditional way of working to the new way of working is actually very easy. And why is that? Because the new way of working is better than the old way. But first, you need to give your people new skills."[43]

We'd add that you need agile coaches to teach these new skills.

These people operate as guardians of the agile way of working, and coach others on how to adhere to it. They work closely with teams, observing every day how team members interact with each other and other teams, reinforcing agile practices, spotting problems, and helping explore solutions. Their aim is to empower others. The team gets the glory.

Agile coaches can't convert everyone. Middle management can prove particularly resistant to agile ways of working—often because their jobs become less important or redundant. In an agile organization, where small teams operate with much greater degrees of independence, fewer people need managing. Not surprisingly, this can lead to significant passive resistance in a transformation program. Addressing the situation requires a delicate hand, but focusing the training on those who are most capable and willing to learn will speed the take-up of agile practices. Fortunately, in an agile team, it soon becomes obvious who the capable people are because of the drive for accountability and transparency. Transitioning crucial

A year in the life of an agile budget

In agile organizations, budget activities occur throughout the year.

▼ **Annual budget**
1 per year
3-6 weeks of preparation

■ **Venture capital funding round (VC)**
1 per quarter
Variable degree of preparation

● **Quarterly business review (QBR)**
1 per quarter
3 weeks of preparation

▥ **Ongoing reviews**
1 per day
Daily activity at the organizational unit level

tasks and initiatives to these reskilled people and teams, and away from the diehards, reduces the negative influence of the latter.

Helping leaders learn how to be agile is important too. The best companies create immersive leadership programs to introduce the new mind-sets and capabilities. They then quickly give program participants opportunities to put their new knowledge into practice by inviting them to take part in agile-transformation initiatives already underway and launching new organizational experiments.

Until leaders take the time to learn about agile, they're not likely to appreciate the value of agility or become its champion. This was the case at a large North American company whose technology organization had been steadily introducing agile ways of working for 18 months. Its efforts, however, had gone largely unnoticed in the rest of the organization. Executives didn't understand what was afoot, referring to it as "that project the technology team is trying to implement." It wasn't until a senior vice president suddenly took an interest, visited the agile teams to see how they worked, and made changes to his own business practices that an enterprise-wide transformation began. Agile was soon identified as one of the company's top-five priorities.

Customer first to the core

Agile is often thought of as a process when it's really a mind-set (supported by processes, of course). Yes, it's about testing and learning, and new ways of working, but at the heart of agile is the determination to provide the customer with something she or he wants or needs. That's the point. Enshrining this principle across the business provides a consistent point of reference. But while almost every company will claim to be "customer first," a closer look under the hood often reveals that internal efficiency or profit rather than customer need is the true driving force.

An agile mind-set starts from the premise that everyone is responsible for the customer, be it the CEO who determines the business strategy, the salesperson directly serving the customer, or the data scientist developing analytics platforms. You will only be able to embed agile ways of working once this becomes a core value, providing cohesion and purpose. This isn't about doing your job better; it's about serving the customer better.

The way a true customer-first ethos comes to life is through design—the process of integrating the customer point of view into all development.

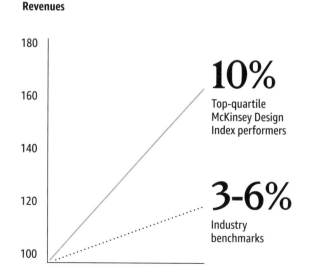

The power of customer-focused design[44]

Companies in the top quartile of the McKinsey Design Index outperformed industry-benchmark growth.

Revenues

10%
Top-quartile McKinsey Design Index performers

3-6%
Industry benchmarks

This is much more than gathering insights or building elegant websites. It's about building an adaptive learning process around the customer for everything the company does.

Getting design right is worth a lot. Companies in the top quartile of the McKinsey Design Index, which rates companies by how strong they are at design, outperformed peers in their sector in terms of growth by as much as two to one.[45]

Here are some of the most important things the winning companies do:

- *They make huge efforts to know the customer.* A design approach requires solid customer insights to understand the real needs of potential users. Yet only around half the companies McKinsey surveyed conducted user research before generating their first design ideas or specifications.[46]

One international pizza chain wanted to improve home delivery, a crowded market where consumers were already spoiled for choice. Data analysis revealed that one of the biggest drivers of customer satisfaction was how hot the delivered pizza was. This fact led the business to invest in "Intelligent Kitchen" technology, which determines when orders are baked based on the delivery address, driver availability, and current location, as well as road conditions to ensure the customer got a piping hot pizza. This approach grew overall sales 7 percent in the first year, and more in the years following.

Prashant Gandhi
Managing Director and
Head of Digital Payments
JPMorgan Chase

The scaffolding that holds chaos at bay

"We know you can't command from the center anymore because the world is moving way too quickly. But while autonomy is much celebrated these days, what's often missing is a careful discussion about the management systems needed to support it. Otherwise, you get chaos.

For me, that management system is based on a shared culture and guiding principles that make clear why we're doing what we're doing. Our guiding principles start with the customer. My teams and I have worked hard to understand what our customers want, which is easy payments, confidence, and value. With that guidance, you can agree with product owners (who

run the product teams) on what the goals are. Then they're accountable for meeting them. I'm responsible for being clear on what the destination is, but it's up to them to figure out how to get there.

This is the scaffolding that supports freedom of action. If the scaffolding is strong, you can get out of the way. If you lay out principles, give people autonomy to deliver on those principles, and provide a system of reviews that's fair and rigorous, people get it and rally around it."

The best results come from constantly blending both quantitative and qualitative research. One top team invites customers to its regular monthly meeting solely to discuss the merits of its products and services. And the CEO of one of the world's largest banks spends a day a month with the bank's clients and encourages all members of the C-suite to do the same.

- *They continuously improve with customer feedback.* Continuous improvement is key to success for a digital transformation. This is the raw learning capability. You can see it in companies that foster a culture of sharing early prototypes with outsiders and discouraging excessive time spent on mock-ups or internal presentations. Despite the value of iteration, however, almost 60 percent of companies in our survey said they used prototypes only for internal-production testing, and even then, only late in the development process.

New technologies allow companies to uncover insights and test products in a dramatically faster way than traditional market research or focus groups. Digital marketing teams can convene online customer panels using video chats and watch as the panels test products and provide feedback in real time. One insurer created digital diaries to help identify customer pain points that would previously have gone undetected. Similarly, digital companies can quickly A/B test new products and campaigns with thousands of customers in hours or days.

■

Food for thought

Agile isn't just a process. It's a mind-set that puts customer objectives first.

Team autonomy works best with guiding principles about what needs to be done and why.

Agile coaches are necessary to train people to learn new skills fast—leaders included.

Agile budgeting helps scale agile by quickly allocating money to projects.

Agile ways of working can't take hold unless they are supported by stable processes.

Design thinking is the commitment to completely understanding your customer.

The power of team proximity[47]
Productivity diminishes as team member locations increase.

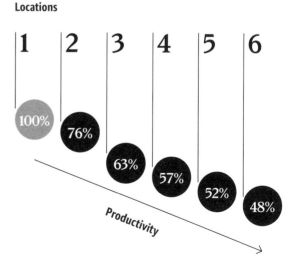

Locations

Have you hired digital stars?

8

Quality trumps quantity when it comes to finding talent. And great talent attracts great talent.

One European CEO, a big football (soccer) fan, pointed out that if you gave him a large enough budget, he'd be confident he could put together a winning football team. But a cricket team? He wouldn't know where to start since he knows nothing about the game.

He used the analogy to point out how hard it can be for company leaders to build an ace digital team today. Getting digital talent on board is difficult enough, given the shortage of supply in a white-hot market. But it can be harder still to identify the right talent in the first place. If you don't know what "good" looks like, where do you begin?

Research suggests getting the right people matters a lot. In highly complex occupations (the information- and interaction-intensive work of managers, software developers, and the like) high performers are an astounding 800 percent more productive.[48]

So it's not surprising that the talent issue causes anxiety in the C-suite. A McKinsey study of more than 300 senior leaders in the industrial sector identified "capability and talent management" as the area where the gap between expected impact and business readiness was largest.[49] That concern plays across numerous types of digital talent, from agile coaches to data scientists. Only 27 percent of respondents to a separate McKinsey survey, for example, said that they had access to talent with the right skill sets to support AI work.[50] Addressing the talent question is particularly hard for big companies, many of which are accustomed to outsourcing large swaths of key capabilities, from IT to marketing.

Focus on getting the best first

To move forward, focus on quality rather than quantity initially. It's true that large companies will need hundreds if not thousands of people with digital skills over time. However, a handful of recognized star performers with the right skills and experience can have an immediate and disproportionate impact on the transformation. (We've seen teams of 10 or fewer high-quality people make remarkable changes. As we mentioned in the book's introduction, a 3-person team carried out a microsegmentation of the customer base at a US telecom company that lifted the efficiency of the company's targeting by more than 40 percent while halving its digital-marketing spend.)

You will need to pay a hefty premium for these rock stars. But the very best people will be well worth the price. In transformations, a core of exceptional talent acts as a nucleus that will ignite change. The stars know what good looks like (and what bad does too) when it comes to hiring more people. They have networks. And they can be magnets for successive waves of high-quality talent. As Red Adair, the famed engineer who built a career around capping oil well blowouts, said, "If you think it's expensive to hire a professional to do the job, wait until you hire an amateur."

Bear in mind, too, that the premium you pay for this initial set of people can temper the salaries of other recruits who are eager to work with top talent. One large retailer determined it needed 11 people to get a signature initiative off the ground, and identified the people it wanted at a leading tech firm. It paid a 100 percent premium to lure them away—but the next 50 recruits, eager to work with the first big-name hires, came for a more modest 20 percent premium. In less than nine months, the team had generated $1.4 billion in additional annual revenue online, a massive payoff.

Raising the quality bar

Beth Galetti
Senior Vice President
of Human Resources
Amazon

"We want every hire we make to be better than half of the people currently working here at that level. One of the ways we work to ensure that happens is through our Bar Raiser program. We carefully select tenured Amazonians to be Bar Raisers who serve as a neutral third party on the interview loop, meaning that they're not in the hiring manager's chain of command. Their purpose is to inject 'tension in the system' to ensure that hiring decisions are made in the best long-term interests of the company. The Bar Raiser is particularly important when a team is eager to fill an open seat and acts as a counterbalance to the hiring manager's need to move quickly. For an offer to be extended, the Bar Raiser must agree to hire the candidate."

Know what you're hiring for

Besides hiring the best, make sure hiring decisions take into account the problems you need to solve not only now but in the future. In a McKinsey survey, companies that set hiring goals based on specific needs were twice as likely to report successful transformations as those companies that didn't adopt that practice.[51] The best organizations measure and track skills development and identify future skills gaps based on a clear view of how the business is evolving, then build a plan to find the people they need ahead of time. Too often, transformation programs grind to a halt as the company struggles to find the talent needed to take the next step.

Melissa Swift
Senior Client Partner
Leader, Digital Advisory
Korn Ferry

Avoiding a compensation arms race

"**Widen pay bands for skills.** Wider pay bands mean a flatter organization—music to digital talent's ears. It also facilitates a greater number of potential lateral moves, which is tremendously helpful to retaining curious lifetime learners.

Adjust the payout mix. Putting more weight on bonuses than base pay keeps fixed costs down. But it also suits many of today's workers, who eschew a steady income in favor of something altogether more exciting.

Get comfortable with bigger pay gaps. If you're paying for value, the pay gap will widen. It's not unrealistic for a rock-star developer to be earning twice as much as the developer sitting next to her.

Set long-term incentives for your most valuable employees. The average tenure of digital workers today is barely 36 months, and shrinking. Tenure for the best is shorter still. For the most important contributors, establish longer-term incentives that will help keep them.

Rethink performance metrics. Find ways to reward the kinds of behaviors that will help your company succeed in a digital world and inspire your people. Project completion rates won't cut it.

Get personal. The more you show you are thinking about the employee as an individual, the more he or she will feel valued, whatever the salary. So be creative with personalized rewards. Some companies help with mortgages or school fees. Others offer to pay training costs for anything, anywhere—an appealing prospect for today's lifelong learners. Others simply offer employees a predefined cash pool to spend on whatever benefits they wish.

Markets evolve, so evolve with them. Eighteen months ago, app developers were hard to find. Today, it's agile coaches who are in high demand. So make sure you are on top of trends and plan accordingly to secure the 'next big thing.' And make sure you don't get locked into unnecessary pay promises. You need 'agile rewards' that retain employees for as long as you need them, and not necessarily any longer. Thoughtful organizations are working to discern which roles will last for 18 months and which for 5 years—and structure rewards to match."

Rethink HR

The HR function in many companies isn't set up for the job of hiring the numbers needed, or the types of people needed. Miguel Peña, the vice chairman of Argentine financial institution Naranja, told us that many potential recruits don't even want to talk to HR personnel because they're viewed as lacking an understanding of what digital really means. They want to talk to the people they will be working with.

The new HR function must be rebuilt from the ground up. Creating a "digital talent war room" is a useful way to make the shift. The war room has an executive sponsor to give it the clout required to bust convention, and a recruiting team immersed in digital culture and dedicated solely to digital hiring. The war room works closely with experts across the business to understand needs and involves them in the hiring process. Its work includes mining new sources of talent, radically shortening the hiring process, and helping craft a value proposition fit for the digital age.

One large US agricultural company established a digital talent war room that completely reinvented the hiring process. Candidates were whisked through screening and interviews, reducing the time it took to make a hiring decision from months to days. Hiring managers consciously cultivated priority candidates during evaluations, walking them through the floor to meet teams and leaders, including the CEO, who made a point of sharing his vision with high-priority hires. The result? In less than six months it staffed an entire skunkworks unit and rolled out a new product after four of those months.

Some HR teams are also using advanced analytics to better learn how to find and retain people, such as identifying which employees are most at risk of leaving the company or assessing the effectiveness of talent pipelines. Those companies that use innovative recruiting tactics—such as having recruits play games or find messages in code, or hosting hackathons—are twice as successful as their peers in recruiting talent.[53] Catalyte, a Baltimore-based software development and AI firm, has gone a step further. It has created a methodology and algorithm that successfully predicts the ability of candidates to succeed as developers. The methodology has also helped remove bias from the evaluation process to increase diversity.[54]

Parlez-vous analytics?[52]

2-4 million

Estimated number of analytics translators needed in the US by 2026

Chief product owner. The chief product owner is the ultimate customer champion. He or she sets an ambitious vision for what is possible across the entire customer journey, then motivates a team of product owners to achieve it.

Product owner. Often described as a "mini-CEO," the product owner is part manager, part visionary, part influencer, part technologist. The product owners are responsible for plotting out what customer journeys look like, and translating that into a product or service that can deliver on it. A good product owner can single-handedly carry a mediocre team. A bad one can bring exceptional engineers to a standstill.

Analytics translator. This role is crucial to help ensure that analytics deliver impact. Analytics translators are a vital connection between the technical experts (e.g., data engineers, data scientists) and operations experts (supply chain, manufacturing). With strong domain knowledge—but not necessarily expertise—translators help business leaders identify opportunities to drive value and convey those to AI and analytics experts. By 2026, the McKinsey Global Institute estimates that demand for analytics translators may reach two to four million.[55]

Lead architect/chief technology officer. Often reporting directly to the CDO or CIO, the lead architect understands how the entire technology landscape fits together, and how it must evolve. He or she also keeps tabs on interconnections with legacy systems and partnerships.

Design lead. The best design lead partners with the product organization to bring the latter's ambitions to life. This person is skilled at teasing out what customers want, where the value lies in those desires, and how to frame them into a consistent design vision.

Agile coach. Agile coaches help squeeze every bit of performance from agile squads. They are always on the floor, helping solve problems, speed progress, and improve team dynamics. They bring agile principles to life.

Chapter lead. Chapter leads are functional leaders within their field, often with management responsibilities. These leaders—be they mobile app developers, application program interface (API) developers, or scrum masters—can emerge from the talent pool organically. But remember, you aren't after great coders. You're after great leaders.

■

Food for thought

Hiring a handful of star digital performers at the outset has an immediate and disproportionate impact on the transformation.

Accept that you will have to pay a hefty premium for digital rock stars, but doing so will help you lure more talent.

Transformation programs can grind to a halt unless you anticipate future skills gaps and hatch a plan to close them ahead of time.

Consider establishing a digital talent war room that reinvents the hiring process and reduces the time it takes to make hiring decisions from months to days.

Is your workforce up to the task?

9

Continuous learning tailored to the specific skills your people need should be at the core of your reskilling program and complement recruiting of top talent from the outside.

The talent challenge is often framed in terms of hiring the right people. That's important, of course. But the reality is that no matter how successful you are at hiring new people, you won't be able to hire enough of them. The demand for new skills is outstripping supply.

Research by the McKinsey Global Institute (MGI) has indicated there will be a shortage of 80,000 workers in IT and electronics jobs in France by 2020, for example, while there's an imminent shortfall of some 250,000 data scientists in the United States.[56]

Some 80 percent of executives think reskilling will be the main way—or as important as hiring—to fill this looming skills gap in the next five years, according to the MGI.[57]

While executives acknowledge the challenge, we've found that their corporate training programs often aren't up to the task. Outdated formats, materials, and programs are too often the norm rather than the exception. And though many companies have rushed to develop e-learning programs or learning apps, these tend to flop because they're unhelpful, irrelevant, or just plain boring.

Becoming an adaptive learning organization means approaching reskilling differently. The best training programs today are:

- **Continuous:** Training events still tend to be time-consuming and periodic, often happening at set times in a person's career. Learning needs to be shorter and happen more often.

- **Lifelong:** The learning journey never ends. Because technology and the world of work change so quickly, people need to learn throughout their careers.

- **Blended:** People learn in many different ways. A hybrid approach embraces a range of traditional and digital formats that reinforce learning.

Here are some of the most important success factors in bringing those principles to life:

Ease of use

Many companies have large libraries of (often out-of-date) content that employees are expected to delve into on their own, or that is served up in dry classes. In contrast, advanced training programs both ensure content is easy to access and provide many more opportunities to learn in short bursts. This approach helps address the number one challenge for talent development, according to a 2018 LinkedIn survey: getting employees to make time for learning.[59]

In the same way that digital technology has led to the unbundling of products (e.g., being able to access single songs as opposed to having to buy complete albums), training programs are being broken up into short, easy-to-use modules for specific tasks that workers can easily access from their desks or on the job. Learning games, e-coaching, virtual classrooms, online performance support, and online simulations are all increasingly in demand. Brief, instructional videos can be effective, while some companies award "micro-credentials" and badges to those who have learned a discrete skill.

AT&T awards "Nanodegrees" for completing a course to achieve a certain skill. Gaining a set of them can help workers move to new roles.[60] A programmer who wants to become a software engineer, for example, typically needs to complete 25 courses. To develop skills in IP networking, she or he needs to complete eight courses.[61]

Digital channels play a key role in making content easy to use because of their ease of access and because young people joining the workforce are so comfortable using them. Outperforming sales organizations, for example, invest in mobile application modules because sales reps are 50 percent

Closing the skills gap[58]

Here's how large companies (>$100m in revenue) that rank the skills gap as a top-ten priority plan to address it:

1%
Only by retraining

40%
Mainly by retraining

15%
Mainly by hiring

3%
Only by hiring

41%
Equal mix hiring and retraining

more likely to find them highly effective for learning new skills, according to a McKinsey study.[62] In another example, an Asian global original design manufacturer offers a digital 3-D learning environment at its virtual model factory. This system lets employee participants "see" and "feel" complex equipment deployed at many of the company's plants.[63]

The content has to be easy to find, of course, so companies should invest in thoughtful meta tagging and UX to make sure that finding the content is as simple as a Google search.

Each learning journey should integrate theory, practice, peer engagement, and assessment

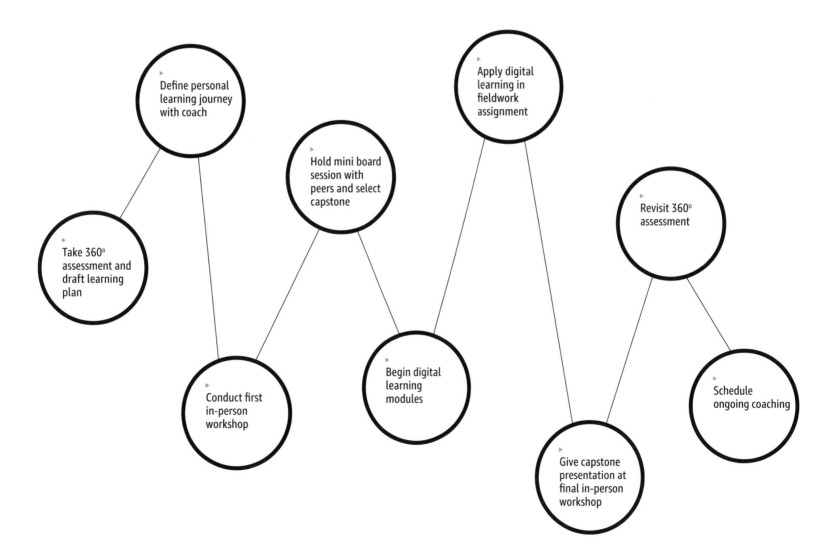

Personal and relevant

The more training is tailored to the person's learning needs, the more effective it is. Top sales organizations, for instance, are twice as likely as others to tailor training by sales role.[64] In recognition of the importance of personalization, AT&T launched the Personal Learning Experience, a tool that helps employees plan and manage their own learning journeys by choosing those courses that are relevant to their ambitions.[65]

F. D. Wilder
Former Senior Vice President, Global Market Strategy & Innovation
Procter & Gamble

Building skills at scale

"At one point, we started hiring external digital talent to accelerate our capability building, but then we realized the biggest tech companies were heavily recruiting our people (around 800 of them) for their commercial expertise. While it still made sense to selectively bring in external hires, we already had great talent and simply needed to invest more in training and development to raise their digital IQ.

As a first step, we created an enterprise-wide Digital Genius Academy (DGA) to upskill the organization. We found that every business unit already had some digital training in place, but there was a wide variation in quality. We started by pulling together the best elements of the training programs from across the company. Then we engineered the content in the DGA to focus on what we had learned over time about the critical few metrics that mattered to deliver business impact, such as winning search, quality content, website health, and superior online fundamentals.

The second program we launched to accelerate the pace of learning was an initiative called 'eyes on consumer, hands on keyboard.' It included access to external coaches and digital practitioners. The problem we were trying to solve was: How do we enable a start-up growth mind-set inside of a large traditional company like P&G?

This program addressed the issue by showing people how to take control of their accounts by putting hands on keyboard to design their own direct-to-consumer website, build their own smart audiences using P&G's proprietary data management platform, post their own creative, and leverage analytics to optimize sales performance. We were teaching people the skills required to acquire new users, convert them to purchase, and retain them for lifetime value. In short, we were moving from traditional brand management to empowered 'brand entrepreneurs.'

More recently we introduced an Accelerated Learning Program (ALP). Think of this as an executive MBA and immersive learning experience. Twice a year we bring high-potential managers from around the world to China to learn about the digital integration of off-line and online commerce ('new retail') and the application of data platforms to grow brand users and drive category growth. Nowhere in the world are consumer expectations changing more rapidly than in China. Online sales are nearly a third of the total business, and China is P&G's largest e-commerce market. The idea behind the ALP is to expose P&G leaders to what's happening in China with the expectation that they reapply their learning to accelerate growth.

The interventions we've made to enable self-directed learning are paying off. P&G now has the highest enterprise-wide digital IQ in the consumer packaged goods (CPG) industry."

The tailored approach applies to leaders as well. When P&G rolled out a training program to raise the digital IQ of its middle managers, it quickly realized that it was the senior leaders who really needed the training. But an open class environment wasn't effective. They needed to give senior leaders an opportunity to dive more deeply into relevant digital topics. To accomplish this, P&G set them up with digital subject matter experts, who were often their juniors in the company, in one-on-one sessions.

"The great thing about this 'menternship' program—where leaders are both mentors and interns—is the learning goes both ways," says Wilder, formerly at P&G. "The digital experts provide the 'know-how,' and the senior leaders provide the 'know-who' to help junior employees connect with the right people to get things done. Everyone wins."

Tailoring the learning experience extends to when as well as who. There are times when people are more open to learning, such as after a performance review or before a specific event, such as meeting a client for a negotiation. Relevant learning modules, therefore, have to be available when needed.

Focused on needed skills

Just as an employee's learning journey evolves, so too does the company's. To keep up with the changes, therefore, companies need a deliberate program to determine the types of capabilities needed to win today and tomorrow, and the skills required to deliver on them. A technology company that recognized the need for a better sales force used analytics to identify the skills that marked its strongest salespeople—in this case an excellent understanding of customer needs and an ability to quantify the value proposition. It then designed specific e-learning modules supported by individual assessments and coaching for weaker performers to build these skills. The new approach delivered a 5 percent quarter-on-quarter sales increase for those reps.[66]

Another tech company developed a new product strategy, and simultaneously identified the new skills required: hard ones (machine learning, IoT, cloud computing, etc.) and soft (agile behaviors, coaching, feedback, etc.). The company determined it would meet half of its future talent needs by reskilling employees, and half from new hires. Within four months, it had designed an internal training program for 10 new career paths in the company. After 10 months, over 1,000 employees had been retrained and 4,000 more were set to undergo training in the following two years.[67]

Targeted funding

One large telecom company decided to invest tens of millions of dollars in a digital transformation, but only allocated $100,000 for training. The result would have been an ambitious digital transformation strategy without enough people having the skills to make it happen (the company quickly realized its error, and significantly bolstered its training budget).

It's hard to put a precise number on what training budgets *should* be since training requirements will differ by industry. Considerable sums need to be spent on teaching compliance in pharmaceuticals or banking, for instance, and training costs are higher in industries where knowledge evolves rapidly. In the digital world, some roles require more training than others. We estimate it can cost anywhere between $5,000 and $10,000 to train a product owner in an agile team, for example. What really matters is focusing on which roles are crucial to drive value, and then allocating enough money to build those skills.

Embedded feedback and coaching

Adults learn primarily by doing. So online or classroom learning needs to be reinforced in the field, often with the help of a coach whose expertise can help employees rapidly gain confidence. One effective way of delivering this kind of experiential learning is to create "learning labs," where the classroom sits next to a model factory or an office. Learners can then walk straight from the classroom into a dedicated work space to put into practice what they've just been taught, whether it's how to work in an agile way or how to digitize a production process.

The best sales organizations embrace this idea through "field and forum" learning. After a training session, sales reps go on customer calls accompanied by senior managers, who provide feedback on key tasks such as relationship building, consultative selling, and account planning, for example. Feedback, in fact, has emerged as an important pillar of continuous learning. Some companies insist on managers providing feedback to their employees daily or as an issue arises, rather than waiting for progress reviews. In agile teams, daily "huddles"—meetings of no more than 15 minutes that were originally designed to identify and address barriers to progress—are often also opportunities for feedback.

Some companies have tools to explicitly elicit feedback. At Amazon, every employee is asked a question each day when he or she logs in to a computer

---

How effective is your capability building?
The right tools can help track progress.

Team barometer: A simple, five-minute survey completed every two weeks that allows any issues with training or coaching to be quickly highlighted and best practices noted

Training tracker: A record of training presenters and attendees that ensures core principles are being taught

Skill matrices: An assessment to track development of both hard and soft skills

Accreditation: A formal evaluation of people's progress

or workstation. "The answers provide aggregated feedback to managers, highlighting areas to improve and surfacing relevant learning assets (such as online training) that the manager can access immediately," said Beth Galetti, Amazon's senior vice president of human resources. "Questions are posed on a wide range of topics, from work environment, to the manager's effectiveness, team dynamics, and, most importantly, any barriers that are getting in the way of employees inventing on behalf of customers."

This feedback approach is increasingly the norm in tech companies. Structured peer review of code and pair programming (where two people write code together) helps to both minimize risk and allow engineers to learn from each other.

■

Food for thought

Learning is a lifelong journey.

Continuous learning is a skill all employees need to develop.

Recognize that adults learn best when classroom learning is blended with experiential learning and on-the-job coaching.

To personalize and scale training, employ innovative delivery mechanisms, such as easy-to-use modules for specific tasks that workers can access from their desks or on the job.

Skills need to evolve with the business, so identify and anticipate them to develop learning programs that address them before they're needed.

Do digital stars consider your organization a career graveyard?

10

Money matters, but you need much more to attract and keep top digital talent.

"It's not you. It's me." That well-worn breakup line may hit a little too close to home for some of us. But it also neatly summarizes a key issue about why it's so difficult to hire the talent you need. You may have impressive HR processes that have pinpointed the AI experts, data scientists, or UX designers you want to hire. You may be prepared to pay impressive salaries (see more on compensation in the chapter "Have you hired digital stars?"). But still you may find that your company's brand or reputation as a "traditional" company is a turnoff for top recruits. The people you want may not want you.

Money matters, of course. Top talent demands top dollar. But other features matter a lot as well—and sometimes even more. Top engineers, for example, cite exposure to technologies and opportunities for professional development to be among the primary reasons for choosing an organization.[68] Korn Ferry research shows how culture has shot to the top of the list of reasons why a candidate chooses a particular company. And a RiseSmart study found that 84 percent of employees would consider moving to an employer with a fantastic reputation even without a big jump in salary.[69]

Companies therefore need to think long and hard about what their target recruits value, and build an employee value proposition (EVP) that will both attract and retain them. Your EVP should help to attract the roles that matter most. If data scientists are a key target, for example, you'll want an EVP that promises opportunities to innovate and invent; offers a clear, rapid career progression; and helps them have big impact.[70] Engineers may value a path that leads to senior salary levels and provides the ability to contribute to open-source technologies.

Even with the best EVP, you will have to accept a degree of attrition. The average tenure of digital workers is barely three years—and shorter still for the top performers lured away with ever-higher salaries. But without a strong EVP, your chances of getting the people you need are low.

Here are some of the most important elements of a good EVP:

Meaningful and flexible career paths

If people management is compulsory for promotion, many committed practitioners—data scientists, AI developers, or designers—will want out. The best companies, therefore, create specific career paths for these kinds of "nontraditional" talent. That can mean giving people more independence and *less* managerial responsibility as they rise through the organization, perhaps letting them do independent research, for example, or assigning them to projects that most excite them.

The best also build more flexibility into the way people can progress along those paths, such as promoting them to more important projects, rather than giving them bigger teams. Some companies have instituted rotational programs that move analytics talent into both business and technical roles. Making job opportunities easier to find and easier to apply for can also signal a commitment to providing people with flexibility in setting their own career paths.

It's also important to integrate key talent. If you hire a top data scientist, and then put her in the back room "taking orders" to crunch code, you're not going to keep her for long. So give the best people opportunities to work in teams with key decision-makers, making clear you recognize and value their contributions.

When it comes to recognition, give a thought to the software development model too. Companies that decide to program their systems in open source say they find it easier to attract and retain top programmers. That's because working in open source not only builds a company's credibility but also helps engineers build their own reputations as they can showcase what they have developed.

Cutting-edge training and development opportunities

The best employees want to keep learning, often acquiring new skills that aren't immediately pertinent to their roles. So, work to understand their goals and help them achieve them by providing a range of learning opportunities both internally and externally. And show that you're serious about providing opportunity by turning to internal talent first when you have roles to fill.

Over the years, P&G has developed a track record for providing its employees with important business skills that prepare them to lead their own businesses later. Amazon simplifies processes to make it easy for employees to expand in their roles, switch roles, or switch locations in an effort to provide them with a rich set of work experiences. Strong mentorship programs that team relatively junior people with senior managers can be particularly effective (for both groups of people). (Read more in "Can everyone in your company easily access everything your people have learned?")

An engaging work space

It will be challenging to attract the best people if they have to work in cubicles or cramped offices that constrict the flow of people and make it hard to collaborate. A key part of your employee value proposition will be offering a creative and practical physical working environment. (The clubhouse for the Golden State Warriors in the early 2000s was so cramped and austere that it was known to discourage visiting players from ever considering joining the Warriors.) Here are some tips:

- **Don't design in a bubble:** Bring in outside designers to get creative, and involve teams in the design so they feel it's theirs.

- **Keep it moving:** Avoid permanent walls and immobile desks and cabinets wherever possible to keep the space flexible.

- **Break the rules:** Don't enforce the same color palettes you've used before. Allow posters or art on the wall, and make sure there is plenty of natural light.

- **Make it work:** A working space is not just desks, chairs, and meeting rooms. Provide whiteboards or glass surfaces, quiet nooks, and spaces where people can congregate and share ideas.

- **It's the little things:** Splurge on decent coffee, soda, and snacks, markers that work, and notebooks people will use.

Location, location, location

One aspect of the EVP that is often ignored is geographic location. Your current location may be a great place to raise children, or it may be close to the shipping lines that once supplied your factories. But if you're not near one of the digital hubs that are home to ecosystems of universities, talent, entrepreneurs, and digital-first companies, you may struggle to attract the right talent. Amazon, for example, makes it a practice to open offices where they find a good source of a specific type of talent. Moreover, moving to a high-profile hub can send a powerful signal to the marketplace that you are all in for building a 21st-century workforce.

The downside of relocating to a hub is that you will need to compete harder for talent, pay more, and accept higher turnover. There is no one right answer here—the balance of pros and cons will be different for each company.

Neil Griffiths
Vice President,
Global Brand, Marketing
and Communications
Korn Ferry

The importance of being authentic

"Too many companies paint a false picture of themselves, creating a value proposition based on a future ideal state (or even a false one) rather than a combination of aspiration and reality. The exaggeration will inevitably be revealed, resulting in rapid exits and a bad reputation that can harm future recruiting efforts.

Finding the sweet spot covering both current and aspirational traits requires in-depth research and analysis. Employee surveys, focus groups (internal and external), leadership interviews, competitor analysis, and social listening will uncover rich data that forms the building blocks of a new employee value proposition (EVP)—as well as guidance on what needs to change and what needs to be better communicated and to whom.

Vodafone, the world's second largest mobile telecommunications company, exemplifies how the effort pays off. Eager to revamp its EVP to attract more female IT leaders in a heavily male-dominated industry, it first identified the profile of the ideal candidate if the company was to fulfill its business strategy. People are attracted to successful personalities—authentic achievers who are also able to drive cultural change. So besides finding people with technical skills, it sought ambitious people who wanted to take control of big projects and didn't need to be told how to operate. It then dug deep to understand what it was about Vodafone that excited its existing female leaders. They held different views, but common themes emerged— the essential, unifying thread of an EVP that ensures it is both consistent across regions and authentic for a fully diverse workforce.

These themes included the company's brand and the ability to work internationally, as well as newer attributes that went unappreciated by many potential recruits, such as the company's leadership in IT, female-supportive work policies, and a fast-paced environment where constant innovation was needed and rewarded.

The repositioned EVP, brought to life through different channels, resonated. Vodafone has not only hired 20 new senior women IT leaders in five countries in less than two years but also identified more than 1,000 women who could be the source of future hires."

Inspirational mission

Make sure your company has a mission that employees can get behind. We've seen candidates and new hires take significant pay cuts to join organizations that communicate a cohesive and inspiring story about their digital transformation and vision.

Miguel Peña, vice chairman of Argentine financial institution Naranja, learned the importance of this when the bank struggled to get top digital talent to even return their phone calls. Only when it focused on telling its story in a way that would inspire people did the tide turn. "We really want to help people by giving them physical and digital products that help them to live their everyday lives easily," Peña said. "That statement helped us to start discussions with top digital people."

Authenticity

In their efforts to revitalize the brand and make it attractive to digital talent, companies can sometimes make false promises that new recruits will quickly spot, prompting them to walk back out the door. A large US public institution, for example, promised interesting work, on-the-job development, and a flexible career path. Lots of people were hired, but when the promises didn't pan out, many of them walked right back out the door.

■

Food for thought

If your recruiting brand doesn't resonate with digital talent, you will struggle to meet your hiring needs.

Inspire: The best talent often wants to do something that brings fulfillment and a sense of purpose.

If recruiting promises don't match up to reality, you'll soon lose your best hires, so make sure evaluations are linked to stated values and provide cutting-edge training opportunities.

Top talent is looking to grow, so your organization needs to provide opportunities to learn and develop important skills.

Do you know how to use new tech to rebuild your core IT and data platforms?

11

Technology has evolved to a point where it's possible to decouple platforms and create microservices that are modular and easy to fix or replace at pace.

Imagine a modern-day Formula One team that chooses to seat its driver in a race car from the 1990s. It could hardly expect to beat anyone on the track today. Unfortunately for many incumbent companies, their core IT systems are the equivalent of a '90s-era racing car.

Long-standing customer-relationship-management (CRM) or enterprise-resource-planning (ERP) systems might have offered stability and solid performance when they were first installed. However, over time, demands on systems have resulted in growing complexity with new functionality continually added. Now the once-helpful platforms have become rigid leviathans, with layers that might be 15 to 20 years old, thousands of lines of custom code written in bygone languages, and countless work-arounds. They're costly and cumbersome to maintain, let alone to integrate with modern solutions.

The emergence of an array of new technologies has made this complex patchwork not only increasingly outdated but also unnecessary, in the process fundamentally changing some long-held beliefs about best practices in technology.

A nuanced approach to platform renewal

Although it is possible to build new solutions on legacy technology stacks, the burden of maintaining and working around legacy tech will consume money and manpower that might otherwise be devoted to boosting productivity or pursuing innovation. In many cases, it is advantageous to build new solutions on modern technology stacks instead.

For this reason, companies should push for simplification and end-to-end renewal across those systems that drive business value by both applying DevOps extensively and providing developers with the rights and capabilities to deploy applications within a well-defined architectural framework. That approach will result in an IT platform capable of powering the rapid learn-and-adapt model of digital winners, allowing for multiple production releases per day and frequent upgrades to new technologies.

While end-to-end renewal is ideal, a dose of reality is necessary. There will be a transition period where new and old systems work together for a time. For this reason, it's also worth spending time on legacy systems, from which plenty of value can be extracted. What we often see is that by systematically cleaning up core transaction systems, removing redundant functionality, and simplifying processes, significant system improvements and cost savings are possible.

One area where this targeted hygiene approach can drive a lot of value is in data-cleansing initiatives, which are crucial for extracting value from AI and advanced analytics. McKinsey estimates that companies may be squandering as much as 70 percent of their data-cleansing efforts.[71] That's because these data transformation programs tend to embrace a "do-it-all" approach. Greater impact comes from working with IT and BU leads to identify which data is needed to deliver on the most valuable use cases.

This focus on value bears emphasizing. It needs to be at the foundation of any tech or analytics program. When it comes to developing a data platform, for example, we often see companies create data lakes without first knowing how they want to use them, resulting in wasted spend (often millions of dollars) and time.

To avoid this trap, we recommend borrowing a well-known phrase popularized in the film *All the President's Men*: "Follow the money." It's easy to get lost in the data—every company has lots of it—so we recommend starting with identifying the sources of value. For an agriculture company, that could be, for example, improved yield productivity or customer experience. For an airline business, that might be optimizing operations or increasing customer share of wallet. Working back from here, the best companies identify use cases and the data sources needed to deliver on those use cases. Teams can then "work" the data (i.e., acquiring, cleaning, managing the data so it can deliver on the designated use cases).

An overview for flexible data platform

APIs should connect disparate data sources and platforms, allowing applications to access the data they need.

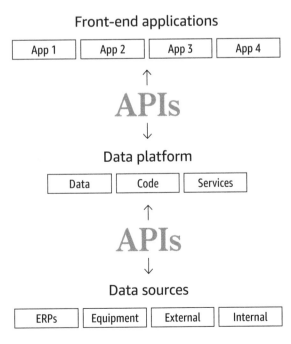

Whatever the approach, technology renewal cannot stop at the edge or only happen for selected parts. The goal needs to be for tech modernization to expand to transform the core systems. While executives might understandably be gun-shy about developing another platform—having often been burned by expensive and time-consuming IT transformations in the past or worried about the risks to legacy systems—technology has evolved.

We're now at the point technologically where it's possible to relatively quickly build self-contained services consisting of small components, such as microservices, that are easy to fix or replace without affecting other applications or systems. Crucially, these self-contained components can include off-the-shelf, open-source, and other third-party solutions linked by open APIs.[72]

Gradual versus radical action

For most companies, it is practical to renew core technologies gradually. One large North American bank chose this approach because the interdependencies between systems had made making changes slow and expensive. The bank's executives opted to build a modular "bank-as-a-service" platform in which new applications, including third-party software, could be quickly integrated to meet new business demands.

In practice, this meant breaking the platform into a set of microservices and moving noncore functions into third-party applications on the cloud. IT leaders prioritized core components for modernization according to the following criteria:

- the extent to which modernizing the component would enable faster, more reliable application development to unlock business value across the bank;

- the extent to which modernizing the component would prevent failures, outages, and other operational problems;

- the potential cost savings associated with replacing the component.

Once the modular platform supplied a majority of the applications, complexity went down and the cost of making changes to core IT systems dropped by 30 percent. More important, the platform greatly shortened the time to market for new digital products and services, typically from more than 12 months to just 3 or 4 months (and even less time in the case of smaller changes). This allowed the bank to respond better to customer needs—its customer satisfaction scores went from average to market leading—and quadruple its revenues from digital offerings, from less than 10 percent of total revenues to more than 40 percent.

In some cases, this gradual approach is not feasible or advisable, and more radical action is needed. This "big bang" approach requires ample funding and the ability to rapidly build technology capabilities. One large retailer sought to rebuild its core IT systems all at once after determining that it had no time to lose: frequent system outages were causing the company to miss out on $1 billion a year in sales.

Hoping to avoid a massive IT investment, executives first considered fixing the 20 or so systems that accounted for the majority of failures. They soon discovered that the integration of these systems with others—some 1,300 systems in all—was so complex that even supposedly targeted fixes would require extensive modifications elsewhere. That led them to pursue a total rebuild.

The rebuild proved surprisingly economical. The first-year investment—establishing a new technology team outside the central IT department, for the sole purpose of building the new core—was less than the annual cost of running the legacy core. The new IT core not only cost much less to operate but also enabled the business to recover quickly from failures and easily integrate new solutions.

Whether companies choose gradual renewal or aggressive wholesale replacement, we find that the key determinants of success are the ability to take a strategic view of where the real value lies across all of IT and a commitment to go after it. Ambitious shifts in technology deployments need to be managed across IT and not just in the "sexy" digital channels, which means, for example, investing in capabilities such as automation and security.

For IT operations, that means prioritizing adoption of cloud technologies and migration of legacy applications to new public or private platforms. And for application creation, IT developers need to think in terms of making applications and services usable by a large number of end users without requiring additional development.

Food for thought

The approach to end-to-end IT renewal varies from gradual to radical. While a gradual module-by-module path to renewal can be effective, it's crucial to keep driving toward the end goal of modernizing core systems.

The all-at-once approach to rebuilding core IT requires ample funding and a strong digital workforce.

New technologies should be developed and deployed to modernize the IT core system.

Technology has now evolved so companies can quickly build platforms consisting of small components that are easy to fix or replace without affecting other applications or systems.

Platform renewal needs to be based on a clear understanding of where the business value is.

Are your own people developing your most important tech?

12

Technology and data are at the heart of any digital business. You simply can't afford to outsource the management of these core assets anymore.

In the rush to outsource functions, many businesses have chosen to assign significant shares of their technology work to external vendors. Some senior executives outside IT see no reason to reverse that trend: more than 4 in 10 say they believe third-party IT service providers can act as a significant or complete substitute for corporate IT functions.[73]

We think this needs to change, because it's getting tougher for tech vendors to give large companies what they need most: the flexibility to learn and adapt at speed.

This "build-it-here" approach is a key characteristic of successful digital companies. Some 52 percent of the most digitized companies build AI capabilities in-house, for example, compared with just 38 percent of other companies, according to a recent McKinsey survey.[74] Top-performing companies are also more aggressive in building up their capabilities by buying, acquiring, or hiring it. On average, top-performing companies use 30 percent of their M&A investments to acquire digital capabilities, compared with just 24 percent for other companies.[75]

Insource versus outsource

One challenge is that because technology is changing so quickly, IT vendors often struggle to bring their clients up-to-date ideas or capabilities that match their needs. Another is that digital companies are agile and intensely collaborative. They refine their operations and their technologies in tandem, over short test-and-learn cycles. Managers and developers—ideally sitting side by side—work closely together on reviewing and updating digital solutions. Most tech vendors just aren't set up to work like this.

In addition, companies are having to make different choices about where to get core technologies. Years back, there were only a handful of companies capable of providing integrated solutions for application support. The main strategic decision that companies had to make was which kind of ERP or core system transaction platform they would use, and only a few major credible suppliers existed. In today's world of modular technology, companies must make more choices about which software components to use, and there are dozens of potential vendors to evaluate.

Top-performing companies devote more of their M&A budgets to acquire digital capabilities and businesses[76]

Acquire digital capability

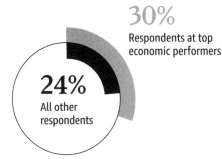

30%
Respondents at top economic performers

24%
All other respondents

Acquire digital business

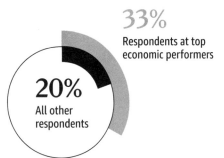

33%
Respondents at top economic performers

20%
All other respondents

Acquire nondigital business

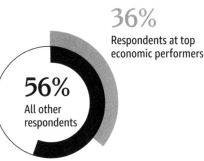

36%
Respondents at top economic performers

56%
All other respondents

It can still be practical for large companies to have IT contractors perform tasks that are repetitive and well defined, such as maintaining stable components or developing software according to precise specifications, without the need for experimentation. But most companies will benefit from building their own tech capabilities in those areas that contribute the most to creating and deploying digital solutions, driving differentiation, and capturing incremental value:

- **Enterprise architecture**, to maintain a current, iterative view of how technology supports the company's operating model

- **Application development**, according to agile and DevOps approaches, to stimulate innovation in software creation

- **Data science and engineering**, to enable companies to extract crucial business insights (e.g., predictions) from a wide range of sources and to make data accessible for business purposes

- **Experience design**, to ensure that new and differentiated digital solutions are created with customers and users in mind

Leaders have not pursued talent transformations as much as other types of transformations[77]

Types of transformations pursued by organizations in the past two years.

63%
Modernizing infrastructure

52%
Redesign of IT or operating model

51%
Digitization

44%
Changes to IT's delivery method

42%
Simplifying architecture

27%
Talent strategy

Renewed focus on talent

To take back control of technology, companies will need to get better at hiring and managing digital talent. This includes developers who are capable of modernizing or rebuilding core system components and agile coaches to help small teams learn new ways of working.[78] This influx of talent will then also require incumbents to scale and modernize their training programs (for more on this, read the chapter "Is your workforce up to the task?").

A European bank, for example, has found that newly hired developers need a full year of training before they can work with the bank's credit engine. But companies should be cautious against simply hiring more tech talent. Tech winners, in fact, have applied a consistent people strategy that favors smaller teams of better talent. For this reason, they focus specifically on hiring top engineers, who generate disproportionate impact through the technical products they develop. Reduction of team size also leads to reduction of support personnel, which further drives down costs and increases productivity (analysis shows that the productivity of a top engineer is eight times greater than a novice though our own experience suggests the number can be much higher).

Talent management, however, has emerged as a gaping need for IT leaders. Just 27 percent of all respondents say their companies have pursued large-scale change efforts in recent years to transform their talent strategy, a much smaller share than those that have pursued digitization (51 percent) and the modernization of infrastructure (63 percent).[79]

TDC, a large telecommunications company based in Denmark, illustrates how profound this kind of staffing shift can be. Before TDC launched the digital transformation of its B2C business, it assigned three-quarters of the organization's IT work to local and international vendors. Recognizing that heavy reliance on vendors would slow the pace of transformation, executives called for bringing the B2C business's IT capability *entirely* in-house.

TDC kicked off its insourcing drive by hiring essential specialists: product owners, microservices engineers, scrum masters, and user-experience designers. Besides advertising these jobs, recruiters discovered candidates by looking at talent magnets like GitHub and developer interest groups and hosting events such as hackathons and JavaScript meet-ups. They also relaxed their hiring criteria, dropping requirements for telecom-industry experience so they could consider a wider pool of talent.

Next, recruiters invited TDC's high-performing developers and system architects in its contractor network to apply for in-house jobs. That tactic yielded numerous hires, because contractors relished the chance to continue working on the kinds of stimulating projects that TDC had been giving them. Within 18 months, the B2C business had brought three-quarters of its IT staff in-house—inverting the ratio from the start of its transformation. All the remaining contractors are based locally, so they can work side by side with TDC employees as full-fledged squad members.

■

Food for thought

It is challenging for tech vendors to give large companies what they need most to differentiate their offerings: the flexibility to learn and adapt at speed.

Companies will benefit from building their own tech capabilities in the areas that contribute the most to creating and deploying digital solutions, such as enterprise architecture and experience design.

It can be practical for large companies to have IT contractors perform tasks that are repetitive, are well defined, and don't need experimentation.

Prioritize the hiring of essential specialists, including developers who can modernize or rebuild core system components, agile coaches, product owners, and microservices engineers.

Is cybersecurity part of your IT transformation team or simply a control function?

13

A security breach can derail your organization overnight. This risk needs to be managed at the core of the everyday operation, not as an afterthought.

A popular saying states that there are two types of companies: those that have been hacked, and those that don't know they've been hacked. And things might be getting worse. Each year hackers penetrate a large number of corporate security systems, and there is no end to the new variants of malware.

That results in millions of dollars in losses, hits to stock prices, and countless days and weeks spent addressing the attack, which pulls resources away from other parts of the business. Almost half of customers in a recent survey from CA Technologies, in fact, said they stopped using a company's services if it was involved in a breach and instead moved to a competitor.[80]

Cyber risk is becoming an ongoing battle as companies embed new technologies into more of their operations and build digital links to applications, servers, and other devices, which expand their "attack surfaces." In addition, companies face increasing regulatory requirements related to cybersecurity, such as the EU's General Data Protection Regulation (GDPR).

New pressure on cybersecurity

These trends have put immense pressure on enterprise cybersecurity teams. They not only are being asked to protect the business against increasing cyber risks and to ensure compliance with regulations but also face new demands from developers and digital specialists to complete security reviews as rapidly as new applications are being built, launched, and updated.

The natural response is to establish tough cybersecurity reviews and approval requirements. The much-needed cybersecurity team instantly becomes a bottleneck for digital transformations. We've seen numerous companies postpone the adoption of new solutions because they aren't sure that their cybersecurity protocols will keep them safe. Or, even worse, they've trampled over security concerns to get a product out quickly. Some 85 percent of respondents to the Digital Transformation Security Global Survey say that business users "avoid engaging with security teams out of concern that their initiatives might be blocked."[81]

This is shortsighted and dangerous. One financial institution that was driving a digital transformation had been making great progress. Software releases went from one every two to three months, to one every two to three days. However, the pace of work was not matched by an increase in cybersecurity protections. The firm was hit with two security breaches, leading to significant bad publicity and massive delays as the teams tried to stop the attacks.

Four adjustments

Four key adjustments can make a decisive difference in protecting a company's digital transformation while still maintaining a rapid test-and-learn posture:

Involving cybersecurity leaders in transformation planning. If the head of security or CISO (chief information security officer) doesn't have a seat in executive meetings about the digital transformation of the company, it is at risk of transformation slowdowns. The cybersecurity leader should be in a position both to shape how the business is changing and to keep cybersecurity capabilities and methods aligned with the company's needs.

Integrating cybersecurity into development. Digital-native companies large and small, as well as some transformed incumbents, operate without quality-assurance teams testing code. Instead, they hold their development teams responsible for seeing that their products meet cybersecurity requirements. Under this approach, each development squad must write secure code, test it frequently, and fix vulnerabilities.

To make this process easier and more reliable, the cybersecurity team works with developers to create automated tools that developers can then use to perform routine cybersecurity checks and flag any issues. Cybersecurity specialists also assign operational security tasks, such as the deployment and release of new products, to developers.[82] Best practice includes developing metrics (such as vulnerability and customer satisfaction scores, and applications that complete key cyber processes) to keep tabs on progress and help report on security.

Making cybersecurity part of product development speeds the process

Security phase gates eliminated at each phase of the process.

Architecture and design

Developers with architecture-security expertise design more secure architectures from project inception.

Architectures are approved for faster implementation.

Implementation

Developers with secure coding expertise introduce fewer vulnerabilities.

Modular security components "snap in," with no need for design implementation.

Deployment

APIs for creating production environments include functions to specify secure configuration.

Configurations are done securely with strong encryption and authentication.

Code review

Secure code scanners conduct automated code reviews for common vulnerabilities.

Developers with secure coding expertise locate and eliminate vulnerabilities before they can be accepted into the code base.

Testing

The team's own developers create and automate test cases.

Developing tools and practices to better defend. While security policies at many companies are robust, they are often not universally backed by preventive and protective controls, standards, or enforcement mechanisms. Technology can increase resilience and help reduce the number of big hits. Better design can limit the damage a hacker can do.

But the reality is that 70 percent of global cyberattacks come from financially motivated criminals who are using technically simple tactics, such as phishing emails.[83] Companies should invest in detection and response technologies so they can more easily track when a breach is happening, and then move quickly to counteract it. In some cases, companies have developed a product assessment dashboard, which gives developers a real-time view on state of security and privacy within products.

Training technology specialists in cybersecurity. Developers simply need to learn more about cybersecurity. While this obviously requires developers to take time away from development work, they usually learn the necessary cybersecurity skills in short order. And the payoff is real. Once developers have acquired new cybersecurity skills, they can cut out the production delays that occur when separate cybersecurity teams need to perform code reviews.

As part of its digital transformation, Aetna, a large health insurer based in the United States, sought to integrate security controls with application development—an ambitious effort that would affect the 3,500-plus developers managing more than 1,500 applications across multiple platforms. To make things more complicated, Aetna's developers were at various stages of a progression from waterfall-style to agile development to DevOps.

Working together, cybersecurity specialists and developers in certain IT domains set up processes for performing cybersecurity checks and threat modeling along with the other routine code tests that were administered during integration and deployment. Once developers and security specialists in those domains had gotten comfortable with the new "DevSecOps" approach, the pace of application deployment increased and the incidence of code defects was cut dramatically.

Food for thought

Digital transformations often increase the "attack surface" of an organization, increasing the risk of a cyberattack.

The need for tough cybersecurity reviews and approval requirements can create a bottleneck for digital transformations.

The head of security or CISO needs to be part of the executive team planning the transformation to educate the group about cyber needs and to ensure smooth security integration with software development.

Integrating cybersecurity teams in transformation planning and development can radically speed up the process by keeping cybersecurity aligned with the company's needs and responding to issues more quickly.

Developers need training to learn more about cybersecurity.

ADOPTION AND SCALING

Is your transformation team filled with change bureaucrats or builders?

14

Traditional project managers cannot scale your transformation. You need people who can build digital products and act as working partners with widely distributed teams.

A digital transformation invites a world of complexity. You'll be fundamentally changing how your company works and even what it does. As any executive knows, managing this change effectively is crucial for a transformation to succeed. But there are some important differences in managing a digital transformation from other transformation programs you may have executed in the past.

The standard expectations of a strong program management office (PMO) are absolutely essential to a digital transformation—planning, tracking, and coordination. The team needs to determine the optimum sequence of initiatives from an efficiency and customer perspective, including identification of any components that can be reused across multiple projects, and address constraints on a ramp-up schedule.

But the nature of a digital transformation demands some additional skills. The leader of a good digital transformation office (DTO), in fact, will operate more like the orchestra conductor, carefully teasing out the best performance from each musician, than the captain of a battleship, issuing orders to subordinates.

The DTO's many roles

A good way to think of the DTO is as a translator between program-level thinking—that is, the overall vision for the organization—and the project-level activities, where individual initiatives are planned and executed.

At the overall program level, the best DTOs overdeliver in a few important areas:

Fleshing out the operating model. To handle the complexity and scale of change within large organizations, the DTO must create a new operating model. Essentially this is a detailed view of how everything is supposed to fit together structurally. This exercise helps the team figure out how to stand up and cluster the base units—cross-functional tribes and squads responsible for a discrete product or service—into coherent groups around a specific value stream (e.g., mortgages for a bank or an account opening for a telco). It allows the DTO to identify both the processes and governance protocols needed to enforce consistency across tribes and squads as well as the mechanisms so HR, finance, and risk functions can effectively support them. A good operating model plan also identifies the KPIs, incentives, changes to capabilities, and the tech and talent to enable it all.

Having a clear view of what the operating model should be matters because it provides a clear goal for what the business needs to build. It helps to align the leadership team and to identify important decisions that need to be made ahead of time (e.g., what sorts of talent or data and tech systems will be needed to support a specific product, service, or process). Without it, there is a significant risk that digital initiatives and agile tribes aren't clear about what the end game is or how they fit into it.

In the absence of a clear vision for an operating model, we've seen companies charge forward with promising initiatives, then 6–12 months later hit the brakes to make major adjustments. That could be, for example, an application that an e-commerce team built out without a clear view of how it works with the in-store operations team, leading to multiple teams duplicating work, using incompatible systems, and confusing customers.

Partnering to solve problems. A fatal flaw we've observed in many transformations is that the DTO will simply create solutions and then try to impose them on the organization. Too often, the DTO is perceived as being filled with "transformation bureaucrats" far removed from the reality of the front line. When this happens, the DTO may generate significant activity, but little in the way of results.

In contrast, the best-performing DTO operates like a service organization that helps teams as they embark on their individual pieces of the transformation. The DTO works with teams, showing them how to use data and results from pilots to make faster and wiser decisions, drive better outcomes, and be more responsive to customers.

Most important, they invest the time with people on the front lines to understand all the relevant details and pain points, and then act as partners to solve problems. That can include, for example, providing resources and expertise to work on an issue, anticipating roadblocks and providing recommended solutions, or escalating a relevant problem to the CEO for a quick decision. As new tools and processes are brought online, the DTO has adoption programs in place so that frontline teams know how to use them.

"We sent lots of developers to work with operators out in the field to figure out how to use the data platform to solve their problems," said Karl Johnny Hersvik, the CEO of Aker BP, who helped lead the development of a data platform. "They created their own solutions, and it allowed them to be part of the development, rather than having something imposed on them from above. And we found that this ended up creating a huge set of advocates, who then trained their colleagues."

An important element of supporting various teams is actively challenging new initiatives, not to squash them but to help teams prepare to drive the program through. In many cases, this means helping them think through the influence model in terms of driving change back in their own BUs and teams. This helps to ensure a program design that's more likely to be successful by thinking through what to communicate, how to role-model the change, and what capabilities are needed. The team helps to identify risks and come up with ways to mitigate them.

A good DTO should have the pattern-recognition skills to anticipate and address problems before they materialize and the judgment to decide whether the right approach is to work through a problem or to pivot to a different solution.

Partnering with leadership. To be effective, the DTO needs to work closely with key leaders in the organization. It's especially important to involve them early and regularly in the transformation so that they feel like part of the team, can provide expertise to drive better decisions, and help to sustain the change after the DTO has disbanded.

While working closely with each function is crucial, the DTO needs to pay special attention to:

- **HR:** The DTO should serve as a high-level digital talent manager, working closely with HR. Indeed, HR should be included as closely as possible from the beginning, ensuring that recruitment and performance management are aligned with the transformation. Together with

Influence model[84]

I will change my mind-set and behavior if . . .

Role modeling: I see my leaders, colleagues, and staff behaving differently

Fostering understanding and conviction: I understand what is being asked of me and it makes sense

Reinforcing mechanisms: I see that our structures, processes, and systems support the changes I am being asked to make

Developing talent and skills: I have the skills and opportunities to behave in the new way

HR, the DTO will map current talent and capabilities as well as future needs, outlining roles and helping to both attract new talent and reskill existing talent.

- **Finance:** It's too easy for finance to become disconnected from the transformation and to be viewed as a onetime savings program rather than a series of ongoing initiatives with results that feed into the overall budget process. So the DTO needs to forge a close relationship with finance, educating the team there on the goals of the transformation and the new agile ways of working. The DTO needs to help finance understand how initiatives unfold and assist them in building a sustainable process to account for the gains or the savings as they are logged.

- **IT:** Technology and analytics are the bedrock of any digital transformation, making it crucial that the CIO/CTO becomes a true partner. The DTO needs to work closely with the tech executive to prioritize and sequence development to support the transformation, identify dependencies (e.g., security needs to be in place before opening a new e-commerce channel), and determine resourcing to provide tech support for initiatives. What's often missed, however, is making sure that the CIO/CTO has a clear understanding of the business and transformation goals so that she or he can be an active part of shaping solutions rather than just "taking orders."

- **CEO:** The DTO has significant decision-making authority, but the truth is that a number of decisions need to be made at the CEO and C-suite level. For this to be effective, the leadership team needs to commit to doing two things: (1) making decisions quickly—winning DTOs will meet with the CEO and executives in the C-suite once a week, and make sure that important decisions are made; and (2) making decisions once. In other words, they must make sure leadership refrains from constantly revisiting and remaking the same decision. Of course, it's necessary to periodically review progress, but this should not be an excuse to revisit and reargue old points. Learn and move on.

Building skills. A digital transformation needs to implant learning DNA throughout the organization. To that end, the DTO also has an important role in overseeing and ensuring capability building. The DTO identifies overall capabilities needed, designs structured programs to develop them at scale, and then tracks progress through certification.

Along with supporting the development of specific skills, the DTO is constantly working to nurture an agile digital culture, using various tools to influence teams to work quickly and collaboratively. To accomplish this,

Success factor:
Continuous improvement

> "Leader took rapid action to devise alternate plans when problems arose."

Survey respondents from companies with successful transformations were

3x

more likely to agree than those from other organizations.

the DTO brings on coaches to teach employees how to work in sprints—the short cycles of development that are the agile unit of work. They work to build solutions to specific issues, and then train people how to use the new tools. They also help teams better understand data, and use it to drive decisions. Through all this, the DTO instills a continuous improvement mentality, showing teams how to constantly adapt products and services to what they've learned in the field.

Building bridges. We cannot emphasize enough how important it is for the DTO to take on the role of bringing together different parts of the organization. Through effective planning, they can see what interdependencies there are and then actively bring the relevant cross-functional teams together, for example IT and marketing when new functionality for the e-commerce site is needed.

In the same vein, the DTO acts as the keeper and conduit for spreading best practices. Sitting at the center of the transformation, the DTO has a bird's-eye view across all initiatives to see what's working and what isn't. The winning DTOs not only capture and codify the best practices but also see where else in the organization they can be applied, and then make them available to everyone, actively sharing them with other units across the business.

Dan Nordlander
Senior Vice President
Western Union

Capability-building teams

"We built the Western Union Way team—WU Way—with 10 high-potential individuals from around the company. So how do you start with that and end up with a fully embedded transformation across a company of 12,000 people? The way we approached it was through capability building. We use the central team for capability building. We'll teach you how to do it, and then you will execute.

As we get the pilots completed, the idea is to turn the team into more of a center of excellence. They'll be there to help you stay on track or course correct when you have troubles. But it becomes more self-driven. And that really enables the scale. That allows us to go from 10 people to maybe 50 in the first wave. Once you get 50 people done, you can do 200 in the next wave.

As the transformation gets embedded into the organization, the businesses start to run their own agile deployments. And the center of excellence is there to keep things on track, to make sure we follow a framework and are tracking the results so that we can measure the impact of the transformation across the whole organization."

When one global telco, for example, wanted to rapidly scale a new agile operating model across different countries and markets, it conducted rapid pilots in one market with the help of the DTO, then used the lessons learned to refine the approach. Once they had a proof of concept, the DTO helped spread the knowledge to new teams.

The DTO is both the catalyst and mechanism for instilling, spreading, and reinforcing digital culture. As it leads teams through initiatives, devising solutions and spreading agile ways of working, the DTO is also amping up the learning capacity of every individual, facilitating and enabling adaptive learning across the organization.

It's important to note as well that this transformation team is temporary. Companies must be vigilant that the DTO does not become another layer in a permanent bureaucracy. In fact, part of the DTO's job from the start is to plan for its own exit. As the organization becomes ever more adept at learning and adapting, the transformation team should fade away. A mark of a successful transformation, in fact, is when there is no longer a transformation team.

Communicating. The DTO functions as the eyes and ears of the transformation and should deliver concise, data-backed reports on all aspects (though it's important not to burden the DTO with constantly developing

Fiona Vickers
Senior Client Partner and
Managing Director of Digital
Korn Ferry

A team of experts

"While the size and makeup of a DTO can vary (10–20 people), it often includes technologists and project managers as well as agile coaches, designers, and data scientists. These are people who are skilled at working with independent teams, translating their needs into business requirements, and then developing and iterating solutions.

Who actually leads the transformation varies by company based on their specific needs. Some bring in a chief transformation officer (CTO), who is often more focused internally on improving the business. Others have hired a chief digital officer (CDO), who generally tends to be more outwardly focused on developing new products and business models. (Another role that is emerging is the chief digital learning officer).

Whoever it is, this person should have the technical skills to manage the transformation as well as the people skills to rally the organization to the digital cause. It requires empathetic leadership and a new inclusive style of working.

Successful CDOs today are marked by their determination to empower others. That characterization can apply as well to the CTO."

PowerPoint presentations and reports for the C-suite and board). In this sense, it operates as the single source of truth on progress, impact, and accountability. This allows the DTO to take on responsibility for the over-all messaging of the transformation program. That includes sequencing messages to the various constituencies—front line, middle management, leadership—at important junctures. This might include an overall message as the program kicks off and follow-ups as the transformation progresses and wins are recorded.

Using remote and digital communications can be highly effective. When senior managers and initiative leaders use new digital channels to reach employees remotely, the rate of success of a digital transformation is three times greater than when they don't.[85] Not to be overlooked, a good DTO bolsters confidence and enthusiasm by highlighting successes. That can include sharing successes at the beginning of meetings (and giving credit), sending regular "heroes of the week" emails or, as in one case, having the CEO call and congratulate big achievers.

■

Food for thought

A strong DTO has to do all the work of a traditional PMO—but go well beyond by working with teams to solve problems, instill a continuous learning mind-set, and spread the new digital culture.

One of its most important jobs is to create a durable operating model that can sustain the transformation well into the future.

The DTO is the control center for the transformation and the source for information, data, and progress. It is, therefore, responsible for communi-cating results to the rest of the organization.

To be effective and to sustain the transformation, the DTO needs to partner with important internal functions, such as HR, IT, and finance.

The DTO should include a range of experts and have a leader who is committed to driving the transformation—not just narrowly developing solutions that may or may not be used.

Can everyone in your company easily access everything your people have learned?

15

All that learning isn't worth much if no one can find it.

There's a saying among executives: "If my company only knew what my company knows." That wistful lament has a ring of urgency these days for companies wanting to become adaptive learning organizations. Too often, solutions created at great expense are used briefly, then lost inside the organization until someone with a similar need comes along and reinvents exactly the same solution—wasting time and money.

Companies already spend millions of dollars on managing the knowledge they create, and it pays. MAKE (Most Admired Knowledge Enterprises) winners outperform peers by 70 percent in terms of total return to shareholders, and 138 percent in return on revenues.[86]

But companies need to be rethinking how they manage both the collection and distribution of their knowledge. Employees are demanding ways to find and use knowledge that's as simple and fast as the applications they use in their daily lives. At the same time, new technologies such as AI and natural language processing are radically transforming knowledge management.

"Because growth is shifting and disruption is accelerating, we have to be the fastest learners, and the fastest at applying that learning to drive the business," said F. D. Wilder, a former senior vice president at P&G. "The key mission of my global team is to disseminate and democratize our learning, because if digital expertise is concentrated in too few people, that's a big risk for the business."

Overcoming this learning deficit is absolutely critical for your transformation. But it's futile to try to do so without supporting infrastructure—and by infrastructure, we mean the technology, processes, and culture to support the free flow of relevant information within the company.

There are two main issues to consider as you think about how to gather and share your knowledge. The first is ensuring that everyone within your organization has fast, easy access to the solutions they're looking for when they need them. The other is developing processes and incentives so that knowledge can spread easily.

Use technology to make it easy

McKinsey research has shown that companies using digital tools and technologies to help employees find what they need are much more likely to succeed in their digital transformations. Key features often include single-sign-on access to databases, a simple process for submitting knowledge, and networking to allow easy-to-use access to various databases.

New capabilities such as semantic search and cognitive computing help to make knowledge more accessible, while social collaboration and gamification tools—such as awards, points, badges, and leadership boards—create more incentives for contributing to knowledge sharing. At one tech company, people had to provide proof that they had shared knowledge to be promoted.

Other companies are creating learning platforms that make finding the right content as easy as locating your next binge-worthy series on Netflix. Indeed, Netflix itself, which makes broad, open, and deliberate information sharing a core value, has a platform that acts as a repository where it constantly logs solutions for future teams to reuse. The company also hosts an internal podcast for sharing important new ideas. If it's easy, intuitive, and compelling, employees in search of instructions, advice, or work-arounds will get in the habit of logging into the company learning platform to find the information they need.

Careem, a car-booking company based in Dubai, has adopted that principle by making the internal performance dashboard available to all. This was a deliberate choice that required the company to address additional security concerns. "We believe that the benefit of driving that hyper-transparency is well worth the costs," says co-founder and CEO Mudassir Sheikha.[88]

It's worth noting, however, that technology is often the source of the

---

Success factor:
Making information available[87]

"Information on everything from customers to financials is freely available to employees."

Respondents from agile organizations were almost

2x

more likely to agree than those from other organizations.

knowledge problem rather than the solution. Enthusiasm for technology to solve all the ills of knowledge access often leads to overly complex solutions that are hard to maintain and rarely used. It's crucial to take a page from design thinking to understand the needs of the end user and develop use cases to address those needs.

Build knowledge communities

"Communities of practice are knowledge management's killer application." That quote is from the American Productivity & Quality Center, referring to the power of forming communities of people with similar roles or interests. Whether they're discussing a new approach to code or a shared passion for ice climbing, they're trading ideas and increasing the overall store of knowledge.

Being disciplined in creating these sharing mechanisms really matters. Effective agile organizations are much more focused on making information transparent, for example, compared with start-up teams, which are characterized by rapid creativity but are often undisciplined in execution, according to McKinsey research.

Spotify has "guilds" that function as affinity groups based on shared interests from web technology to customer-centric design to nanotech. Employees from any team or role can join, gather, or leave according to their interests and knowledge. Even simple activities such as book clubs, a speaker series where you bring in outside experts from diverse backgrounds, or lunch-and-learns where team members present on topics they feel passionate about can help bolster a learning culture. This helps build engagement, connections, and a broader base of general knowledge.

Informal and formal mechanisms to support these communities should be the focus of any learning organization. Some other examples include regularly scheduled calls, peer reviewing of new content and ideas, creating and curating a list of domain experts, and publishing content to an internal platform like a wiki or Slack.

F. D. Wilder, former senior VP at P&G, created a specific program to help spread the ethos of learning. "In order to share knowledge quickly, I launched a thought leadership platform called Fastest Learner Wins. I make the content 'snackable' to address the learning 'barrier': time. Each video episode is fairly short, five minutes or less, and people can watch it anywhere and anytime. About 80 percent of interviews I do for the series

Success factor:
Digital learning tools[89]

"Companies implemented digital tools to make information more accessible."

Survey respondents from companies with successful transformations were

2x

more likely to agree than those from other organizations.

are external—people like Thomas Friedman, Chip Conley, Stan McChrystal—because it's important to get outside voices into our company to gain new insights and benchmark how we are doing. The big idea is to shift our culture from knowing it all to learning it all."

Spread learning through job rotation

In siloed companies, star employees are jealously guarded and moving to other internal roles can be political minefields. Digital companies, in contrast, make it easy to try out new roles and new locations.

Learning happens fastest when the curve is steep; in other words, when talented people spend as much time as possible outside their comfort zones. "We estimate that well over 90 percent of the learning that happens at Amazon comes from being challenged and having new experiences in their jobs," said Beth Galetti, who leads HR for Amazon.

Besides keeping your most ambitious workers refreshed and engaged, opportunities to join other departments or regional offices mean that more people are exposed to more ideas. In fact, companies that are prepared to shift people around are 63 percent more likely to have higher total returns to shareholders than those where talent is static.[90]

Beth Galetti
Senior Vice President
of Human Resources
Amazon

Supporting a culture of information access

"For ongoing learning, we have an internal wiki site that contains a wealth of information about Amazon's peculiar culture. We also have an internal video site called Broadcast, where people can post videos so that others can learn everything from specific coding practices to how to write a persuasive 'working backwards' document. The working backwards process is incredibly important since it guides our thinking as we consider launching new products, ensuring that we never lose sight of the customer experience.

Since we know which videos perform best, we actively curate the content to make the most effective ones easy to find. We also have classes for face-to-face training, but we rely on people to be self-reliant and scrappy by reaching out to get information."

■

Food for thought

The loss of hard-won knowledge due to poor infrastructure and knowledge management can slow your transformation to a crawl.

Communities of practice are the killer app of knowledge management.

Building a robust knowledge infrastructure will ensure that learning is captured, archived, and made accessible to all.

Knowledge management and sharing are partly a technology problem and partly a mind-set issue. People need to be motivated to seek knowledge and then share it widely.

Learning happens by trying new things.

Does your commitment match your bold statements?

16

From making big decisions to giving up control to shifting large amounts of people and financial resources, being digital requires executives to make significant changes in how they lead.

We know how important it is to be bold in driving digital transformations. The media and company reports are filled with pronouncements from executives making clear their aspirational intentions. But while bold aspirations are important, they are worth little if not accompanied by bold actions. And these require CEO commitment.

Commitment often means making unpopular decisions, such as shutting down operations that have outlived their peak years but are headed by powerful executives. Or pulling the plug on new initiatives run by stars that have consumed considerable resources but aren't showing good enough results. Or making a big investment that won't pay off in the short term when shareholders are baying for quick returns. Digital transformations can cost tens of millions of dollars. Breaking even often doesn't happen for at least one or two years, and the big payoff may be even further out.

It was this kind of commitment that fueled Silicon Valley venture capitalist and Warriors' owner, Joe Lacob. He jettisoned a winning coach and traded away a star player for the chance to build a team that could win championships. Though deeply unpopular with many fans at the time, those decisions laid the groundwork for a Warriors team that went on to win three championships in four years.

A litmus test for commitment

Large organizations today face similar trade-offs. Many have made significant strides in their digital transformations, such as launching digital initiatives and investing in modernizing IT systems. But those programs, while improvements, fall short of the kind of change that's needed to win in the digital age.

A CEO's hesitation to commit is understandable given the upheaval and uncertain rewards. CEOs who have been in the job for a number of years are there because they have a track record of being successful. Trying something significantly different—like making a large business as agile as a digital start-up—puts their reputations at risk. That can help explain why so many leaders make public announcements about plans to embrace digital but privately drag their feet. Or why they let underperforming initiatives carry on for too long, green-light multiple (often-conflicting) small initiatives that deplete energies, and sideline major investment decisions.

There are often good reasons for these decisions, but they still fall short of the kinds of commitment needed to deliver a real transformation. While there is no perfect metric to track leadership commitment, the following questions offer a useful litmus test:

- How many times have you, your team, and your board visited high-performing digital companies? If it's less than three, that's a concern.

- Have you not only announced your plans to the market, but also reported on progress every quarter? This keeps the pressure on. Leaders in organizations that report successful transformations are two and a half times more likely than others to regularly update investors and/or markets about a transformation's progress.[91]

- Are you spending at least 20 percent of your working day on your digital transformation? It cannot be a sideshow. CEOs at companies that report successful transformations are almost two times more likely than other companies to spend a significant amount of their time working on the transformation.[92]

- Have you tied performance bonuses for your entire executive team to successful digital outcomes? The CDO or CIO cannot lead this alone.

- Have you shaken up the organization by rotating staff in key positions? Many will feel unsettled initially, but it's a quick, surefire way to break down silos and encourage learning.

- Have you eliminated or otherwise curtailed other large capital initiatives to ensure sufficient leadership attention is devoted to digital? Digital leaders are more likely to divest business lines being made obsolete by digital.[93]

- Have you personally interviewed people for key digital roles and participated in leadership recruiting events? Successful transformations mean pulling out all the stops to get the best digital talent.

- Have you arranged for the board to undergo training to better understand business in a digital world? You'll need the board's support for your transformation, and are unlikely to get it unless it is informed enough to provide good guidance.

- Have you made some big bets, investing in potentially disruptive but still unproven technology to keep your options open? The cautious approach of placing many small bets ultimately starves all initiatives of the resources needed to scale and break through. Some 26 percent of digital incumbents and 28 percent of incumbents moving into new sectors say they have acquired new digital businesses while just 15 percent of traditional incumbents have done so.[94]

A new leadership style

Commitment to a transformation is also reflected in a CEO's willingness to adopt a new leadership style. While it may be true that a rigid command-and-control style of leadership is not effective in running a digital business, encouraging senior leaders to "let go" isn't quite right either.

Instead, winning executives adopt a new leadership approach:

They get comfortable with uncertainty. It is impossible to know the precise outcome of a digital program. That's why creating an organization that learns and adapts is so important. Nevertheless, it can be a rough adjustment for some to make. One CEO at a large retail business asked his CDO, who was building a new business, what he would be doing with the business in six months' time. The CDO said he wasn't certain, because he would have to test, learn, and adjust as needed. There was a vision, but not a step-by-step plan to an exact end state. The CEO was *not* happy with the answer and let his CDO know it, demanding more clarity (the CDO and his team left the business four months later). But it was the right answer for an organization primed to learn and adapt.

The CEO has to set bold targets and lay down plans that guide initial

Digital incumbents invest more boldly than traditional competitors[95]

Percentage of companies that have acquired digital businesses.

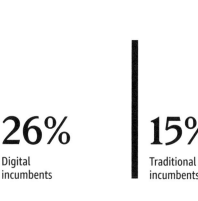

26%
Digital
incumbents

15%
Traditional
incumbents

decisions, such as where to allocate funds. But then she needs to give the digital teams considerable leeway to find the right way forward, learning along the way.

They stay close to what matters. "What can I learn from 15 people?" That question from the CEO of a multinational telecom addressing why he didn't at first visit his small digital team spoke volumes about his commitment to digital. When he did finally visit, he was blown away by the creativity, speed, and value of the work being done. From then on, he visited every week to learn more and understand not just what was happening but why it was working. He saw, for example, how much value the team was generating and realized that he'd way undershot the ambitions for the transformation. So he raised the ambition tenfold, dedicated more resources to the program, and lit a fire under other business units, asking their leaders to emulate the digital team.

Staying close to digital initiatives—from attending weekly progress reviews with the digital transformation office to visiting teams in the field—allows the CEO to understand what's happening, to motivate the business, and to make more informed decisions. One effective way to do so is to ensure the transformation team and its leader—often the CDO—report directly to her.

They empower others but also hold them accountable. Empowering others has been a long-standing virtue of top leaders. But in a digital transformation, empowering others is the key to survival. That's because decisions have to be made more quickly by those who are in the position to know best—often those on the front lines who are far removed from the CEO. A digital CEO takes the time to understand the value of a proposed initiative, what its role is in driving a digital transformation, and what the measures of success are. But then she not only gives teams lots of flexibility to deliver but also provides the necessary support. One of the most important ways a CEO empowers the digital teams is by intervening to break roadblocks, which often materialize when leaders from different functions cannot work effectively together.

While the CEO gives digital teams the space to work, she also needs to hold teams accountable and closely track progress against KPIs. Through regular check-ins—often quarterly—winning CEOs review progress with the relevant teams. The CEO's main role here is challenging the progress to help determine whether to proceed, what resources are needed, and what the outcome should be. If results don't match the promises, the CEO can and should shut down the failing initiative.

Food for thought

Digital transformations demand big commitments from CEOs to changes that will inevitably cause upheaval. Tentative measures will not deliver.

A number of specific actions—from personally interviewing important digital candidates to spending adequate time on digital topics—reflect the level of a CEO's commitment.

Command-and-control leadership won't work, but completely letting go isn't the answer either. The best digital CEOs are comfortable with uncertainty and give their teams space to perform, but they stay close to the action and hold teams accountable.

Are you communicating in a way that's meaningful to your people?

17

Your team will be taking their cues from you. You need to make them believe in the change and empower them to drive it.

One CEO confessed in a private moment that he didn't understand the intricacies of his firm's digital transformation and felt, slightly awkwardly, that he had become no more than a cheerleader. While his discomfort was understandable, he had stumbled on an important insight into a CEO's role during a digital transformation: the need to communicate to and energize the organization.

"Communication is the most important skill any leader can possess," according to Virgin's Richard Branson.[96] While effective communication to stakeholders has always been important, Branson's words have taken on greater urgency for leaders navigating their businesses through digital transformations, which can unleash waves of collective fear, discontent, and doubt.

The CEO and other leaders need to combat that fear by demonstrating unwavering, infectious belief in the new direction. And they do that by communicating well.

Communicate progress and success

Our research suggests that good communication—particularly about progress—is often perceived as the single most important ingredient of a transformation.

> **"Every move you make, everything you say, is visible to all. Therefore, the best approach is to lead by example."**
>
> Joseph M. Tucci
> **FORMER CHAIRMAN AND CEO OF EMC (NOW DELL EMC)**

In our experience working with successful leaders, we've found that they are relentless in finding successes and communicating them obsessively. When done well, this has the effect of not only reassuring often-skeptical employees—most people in a large organization will only know if the transformation is working if you tell them—but also injecting a shot of adrenaline into the organization.

How a leader communicates varies, of course. Town halls are useful to communicate big messages, and announcements by email of important milestones met can be helpful. But beware of overload. Enthusiastic emails, charts, and updates can become repetitive and just plain boring.

Learn to communicate frequently with other stakeholders too—investors, potential recruits, and shareholders. You might even embark on a speaking circuit to trumpet all the digital changes being made, the new business gained, the new hires enlisted, and the savings accrued. In fact, communicating externally can be an effective way of communicating internally.

"I found that the most efficient way to get commitment internally was by showing commitment externally," said Øyvind Eriksen, the president and CEO of Aker Group. "We stated publicly that we at Aker Group wanted to share and collaborate in different ways from how the industry had traditionally acted. Our employees saw this as an inspiring message."

Success factor:
Leadership communication[97]

> **"Leaders communicated progress broadly across the organization."**

Survey respondents from companies with successful transformations were

8x

more likely to agree than those from other organizations.

> **"Leaders were transparent about implications for individuals."**

Survey respondents from companies with successful transformations were

4.4x

more likely to agree than those from other organizations.

> **"Leaders used consistent language to align the organization around transformation goals."**

Survey respondents from companies with successful transformations were

3.8x

more likely to agree than those from other organizations.

The power of role modeling

We've all heard the saying that actions speak louder than words, and that's especially true in a transformation. All the written and verbal communication in the world will fail to get people on board if they don't see you living up to what you say.

Research is clear about the impact role modeling by leaders can have on the success of a transformation. Transformations are 5.3 times more likely to succeed if their leaders role-model the behavioral changes they seek from others.[98]

But leading by example goes well beyond meeting employees on "the factory floor," and praising teams publicly on Twitter. Both have their place, but the effect dissipates quickly, replaced by cynicism. If you never show real engagement—rolling up your sleeves to work on a whiteboard or picking up the phone to speak to someone on the front line if there is something you don't understand—you might find it hard to inspire those around you.

"One of the most important traits typically is 'role modeling,'" said Alain Bejjani, CEO of conglomerate Majid Al Futtaim. "People need to see senior leaders 'walk the talk.' Otherwise, their words lose credibility, and

Success factor:
Role modeling[99]

"Leaders role-modeled the changes they were asking employees to make."

Survey respondents from companies with successful transformations were

5.3x

more likely to agree than those from other organizations.

their ability to inspire and influence is constrained." Bejjani, for example, chose to role-model transparency by sharing his 360-degree feedback with his team.[100]

Indra Nooyi, the former CEO of PepsiCo, would write the parents of employees to thank them for their children to emphasize the need to build relationships within the business.[101] Mudassir Sheikha, CEO of the car-booking company, Careem, spent one hour every week calling customers who aren't using the service anymore to ask why. And there is, of course, the well-known example of Jeff Bezos using a door as a worktable in Amazon's early days to emphasize the importance of frugality.[102]

Investing time in visiting teams can have a similar effect. One CEO of a large telecom company visited his agile digital team weekly. During the visits, he was curious about what people were doing and spent time talking with the team about their work. Not only did this inspire the team, it also inspired other leaders to take notice. Business unit heads from across the company now make the trek as well, and bring ideas back to their teams.

If you are in any doubt as to the power of CEOs to shape perceptions through their conduct—what they say as well as what they do—think only of the tone set by Microsoft's Nadella, who promotes what he calls empathetic leadership, and the importance of listening and collaboration.[103] "When you meet Nadella, you're struck by his interest, how he listens, his humility. As a result, you can't help thinking differently about Microsoft," said a company insider.

F. D. Wilder
Former Senior Vice
President, Global Market
Strategy & Innovation
Procter & Gamble

Raising awareness of successes

"[A] key communication issue is telling our own stories. There was a general lack of awareness inside the company of what we were doing. People just assumed that we weren't doing much or were falling behind. None of that was true. We'd made some massive progress, but people didn't know about it. To raise awareness, we launched a campaign—'P&G is cooler than you think!'—at our annual innovation summit called Signal to highlight some of our own stories.

As an example, one of our scientists, Sara Giovanni, designed diapers for her twins after returning from maternity leave. Like lots of mothers, she wanted an organic diaper with no trade-off on performance. So she worked with a small team of five to six people applying lean innovation principles. They introduced Pampers Pure in 18 months—our normal process took three to five years. Sara shared her experience on Fastest Learner Wins (one of P&G's knowledge-sharing platforms), receiving thousands of views as her story demonstrated both what was needed and possible at P&G."

■

Food for thought

The CEO and other leaders need to combat the fear that a transformation can cause by demonstrating unwavering, infectious belief in the new direction, and providing as much clarity as possible.

Search out successes and communicate them obsessively.

Every move you make, everything you say, is visible to all. Therefore, the most important way to communicate is through role modeling.

18

Are you ready to see your transformation through to the end, no matter what?

Building early momentum is a must for your transformation, but there will be ups and downs to manage on the path to sustaining the change.

When British distance runner Roger Bannister described how he broke the four-minute mile in 1954, he recalled how his legs seemed to meet no resistance.[104] He felt he was flying around the track.

Creating that sense of momentum, having the wind at your back, is crucial to sustaining a digital transformation. That's because a transformation takes a long time.

A company may be able to transfer a good chunk of its sales online quickly, for example, but that won't remove much cost from the rest of the business in call centers or retail outlets. Likewise, legacy IT takes a frustratingly long time to modernize.

Business leaders consistently underestimate the timeline, which can lead to nervousness after about 12 to 18 months and pressure to pull the plug on the transformation or massively scale back. In a global survey, 87 percent of senior executives said they felt under the most pressure to demonstrate financial results within two years.[105] We know of a number of cases where transformation budgets were cut by as much as 50 percent within the first year of the program.

Urging stakeholders to be patient is not the answer. Indeed, while a successful digital transformation requires a long-term commitment, the CEO must be impatient to see progress. Hence, he or she should be constantly on the lookout for the speed bumps that slow progress. Some are well known, such as when the procurement function adheres to its traditional approval process, holding up fast-moving agile teams. Others, however, are harder to spot and trickier to address. Ignoring them, however, can lead to significant resistance in the system, grinding the transformation down to a glacial pace.

Address passive resistance

To many people, the prospect of working in an agile team is exciting. To others, it's less so. That's because they fear change or see their jobs disappearing, particularly if they hold managerial roles. Their fears are often valid. A company that once outsourced all its coding and had dozens of people managing the process won't need many managers in a world where small teams are rapidly writing, testing, launching, and iterating code themselves.

The former executive at a large bank recalled how it was clear at the very outset of his company's transformation that many employees in the IT organization wouldn't add enough value in the new world. "We had many more people talking about coding than actually coding," he said.

Concern about what the future might hold often results in a wave of passive resistance. The counterattack is to focus on the changes that can benefit your people, not just the business. That means setting up agile training courses and insisting that new initiatives adopt agile working practices. The benefits will quickly become apparent to those working on agile teams. They enjoy a great deal of autonomy, they see results fast, they get recognition for their achievements, and they have the opportunity to develop their own skills. (See the chapter "Do you know what it takes to scale an agile culture?" for more on this topic.)

Decisions about people who can't or won't make the shift to the new ways of working, or who cannot be retrained for new roles, need to be made swiftly. The longer a company hesitates, the greater the drag on the transformation. The aim is to ensure every employee working in an agile team is adding value so that the organization moves forward.

Combat transformation fatigue

It's not easy maintaining focus over long periods of time. Initial enthusiasm for the transformation dissipates as people lose focus or even interest. The discipline and commitment that characterized the early days inevitably fades, particularly if things aren't going well. And there are bound to be ups and downs in the course of a transformation, so leaders must be alert to transformation fatigue.

There are a number of slippage indicators. Weekly go-and-see visits to other companies become monthly and then quarterly. Weekly progress reviews become monthly or are increasingly rescheduled. Reports on digital initiatives become less specific. And when the CEO speaks to the board, digital topics slip further and further down the agenda.

Leaders should keep an eye open for these telltale signs, and then be ready to intervene. One effective intervention is to take a step back every six months or so to review how things are going. It's like taking your car in for its regular 10,000-mile checkup. In essence, you're giving yourself the opportunity to take a fresh, honest look at the transformation to see what needs fixing.

Sometimes it's simply a matter of going back to basics. After one of these reviews, a European telecom company reinstated daily stand-ups (where individuals report on what they are doing) and insisted on both more detailed progress reports and greater clarity on who was accountable for progress. The CEO also committed to visiting the digital unit at least once a week.

Sometimes more radical action will be required. More than a year into a transformation, a large retailer had still failed to stop a decline in online sales despite the efforts of various senior executives who had been asked to lead the change. The CEO decided it was time to hire a new CDO from outside the organization. Within two days, the newcomer had started to cut ineffective marketing spend, examine the ROI of all activities, and drive more customers to the website by optimizing search terms. He also kicked off searches for 20 specific digital roles.

Secure and protect funding

The standard approach to protecting funding is to ring-fence it—that is, remove it from the standard budgeting process. But even ring-fenced

The tipping point for a successful transformation[106]

10%

Percentage of people holding an "unshakable belief"

resources can become a tempting target when the going gets tough. So it's helpful to do the following:

Win explicit C-suite and board buy-in. Support from the board and the entire C-suite to see through a digital transformation is an absolute necessity. Make sure the projected benefits are writ large in the long-term plan too. That makes it harder to pull the plug midway, since there will be no other option for delivering the promised value than seeing the transformation through.

Even so, doubts can emerge as time passes, so keep management and the board informed and engaged. It will be hard to protect resources if people don't think the transformation is working. So communicate doggedly, pointing to progress in all its manifestations. (Read more on communicating in the chapter "Are you communicating in a way that's meaningful to your people?")

Establish a transparent governance process to release funds quickly. Even when funding has been secured, accessing it can be a bureaucratic nightmare that slows the entire process. This needs to be countered. A process similar to that used by venture capitalists can help.

A VC-style process ensures that projects only receive a tranche of funding if they have met strict criteria. If they haven't, funds are reallocated to more deserving initiatives. If they have, more funding is guaranteed. Besides helping protect transformation funds, it's a fluid, dynamic process, designed to support the building of an agile organization by assuring funds can be injected quickly into promising initiatives.

One way we've seen this work well is by setting up a transformation advisory board—often a small group made up of board members, the CEO, and someone who understands the market—that meets regularly. The members have the mandate to confirm whether milestones have been met, release funding, and make quick decisions. This approach helps to decouple the normal, often-cumbersome board review process for funding. (Read more about agile budgeting in the chapter "Do you know what it takes to scale an agile culture?")

Measure what matters for long-term success

If you are impatient for results, you need to put performance indicators in place. According to a McKinsey survey, 51 percent of respondents reporting successful transformations said the company monitored KPIs, compared

Success factor:
Monitoring key performance indicators[107]

> "My company closely monitored KPIs to ensure implementation was having the desired effects."

Survey respondents from companies with successful transformations were almost

4x

more likely to agree than those from other organizations.

with 13 percent of respondents at companies where transformations were judged to be unsuccessful.

The question is, which indicators to track, and how many of them? Our research shows that most programs devise too many metrics, and that fewer than 30 percent of them end up being used.[108]

Metrics need to be focused on what you want the transformation to achieve. If you focus on financial gains early in the transformation, for example, you will be setting up many initiatives for failure. Instead, you need to track leading metrics that gauge future growth and longer-term value.

When it began its digital transformation, Schneider Electric, a France-based energy management company, decided to focus on the number of products and devices it had connected to the IoT rather than on the income they generated.

"That decision took a big leap of faith," said Emmanuel Lagarrigue, the company's chief strategy officer. "But using the traditional metrics for judging a new project's potential would have guaranteed nothing got off the ground. Instead, we fueled the transformation because we got people on our side by focusing on different metrics. Now we're ready to set a tougher challenge with a new KPI—the number of devices connected to assets under management. From there, the next step is likely to be a monetary metric."

There are indicators you can track to monitor future growth that look for changes in behavior and pace. For example:

- Customer-centricity (customer satisfaction scores)
- Usage (number of developers that create applications on the platform)
- Agility (time from idea to minimum viable product)
- Time to market tracks how fast you're able to generate new products, services, and business models or make changes to how your business runs. If it's getting faster, you're on the right track
- Internal adoption (percentage of people converted to the new way of working)

Balance the short and long term

The importance of short-term wins in a transformation cannot be overemphasized. They can unlock millions of dollars in weeks or even days if they focus on cutting costs from inefficient processes and putting money

Success factor:
Planning for long-term sustainability[109]

"Planning from day one for long-term sustainability of changes."

Survey respondents from companies with successful transformations were

3x

more likely to agree than those from other organizations.

where growth lies. (For more on this, see the chapter "Do you know what great looks like?") This not only generates funds to fuel longer-term initiatives but also energizes the business and solidifies support among the company's leadership.

But resist the temptation to focus on short-term wins to the detriment of longer-term investments. That's a mistake. As important as short-term wins are, companies that report successful digital transformations are three times more likely to plan for the long-term sustainability of changes than their less successful peers.[110]

Some of these longer-term investments—such as renewing your IT architecture or launching a new product or business—may take 12 months or more to pay off. But they are the mark of incumbent companies that have chosen to compete digitally. Research shows that these companies invest significantly more than traditional incumbents in making big long-term moves: launching new digital business models and new digital businesses (and divesting more aggressively from underperforming or unpromising businesses). Big bets might make you nervous, but they are essential. Remember that for companies focused on the long term, McKinsey analysis has shown that average revenue and earnings growth were 47 percent and 36 percent higher respectively at those businesses we studied.[112]

Digital transformation in a downturn

Given how long a digital transformation can take, business leaders should be prepared to manage through a downturn. While the case law on how to drive a digital transformation through a downturn is limited, we believe there are three lessons from the last recession that can be applied:

Digitize the business processes that are most scalable. To deliver on this, reallocate your best people and build the necessary digital and data capabilities to support these priorities.

Accelerate the pace of the transformation by cutting underperforming programs or businesses. McKinsey analysis shows that the companies in the last US recession that divested aggressively from poor-performing businesses or initiatives outperformed their peers.[113]

Acquire assets. There will be opportunities to acquire good assets much more cheaply. McKinsey data suggests that the best performers make these acquisitions aggressively coming out of the downturn.[114] This requires shoring up balance sheets to fund the acquisitions.

Digital incumbents take bolder actions to succeed[111]

Percent of respondents

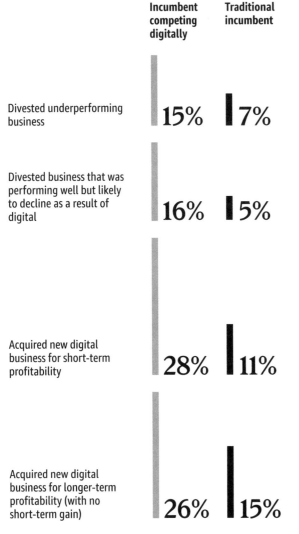

	Incumbent competing digitally	Traditional incumbent
Divested underperforming business	15%	7%
Divested business that was performing well but likely to decline as a result of digital	16%	5%
Acquired new digital business for short-term profitability	28%	11%
Acquired new digital business for longer-term profitability (with no short-term gain)	26%	15%

Companies that have the will and discipline to drive their transformation forward will develop a superior operating model that is more effective and efficient—a crucial asset in a downturn.

■

Food for thought

Transformation fatigue can slowly choke off progress. Establish regular check-ins to take a fresh look at progress, and then decide on interventions.

Employees need to support the transformation or passive resistance will take hold. Provide employees with real training and growth opportunities.

Establish a transparent governance process to guarantee that initiatives get the funds they deserve without excessive wrangling.

Set leading performance indicators, such as time to market, rather than financial ones to maintain focus.

A digital transformation will need a steady drumbeat of wins. That requires a balanced portfolio of initiatives that deliver in the short and long term.

A downturn can provide companies with an opportunity to get ahead of their competitors by digitalizing those processes that are most scalable and acquiring assets more cheaply.

Mudassir Sheikha
Co-founder and CEO
Careem

Investing in the long-term win

"We used to believe that growth was the ultimate proof of success. That was true for the first two to three years when we had little money. But as we grew and started making more money, we realized we were only spending it on growth, rather than capabilities. It was like a drug—we were giving away free rides, for example, to expand our customer base. I came to realize that it is the customer experience that will ultimately drive growth, and so we need to invest in that.

Experience-driven growth takes more time and being in a region where there's no shortage of capital, it's hard when a competitor cuts prices by 60 percent. But we believe in building the experience and are committed to it, so we can weather those challenges."

How much and what have you learned today?

Continuous learning needs to be part of your personal development to keep up with how the world is changing.

Throughout this book, we've talked about the need to implant learning DNA across the organization. An adaptive learning organization should be filled with adaptive learning people—and that includes you.

Wanting to learn is all well and good. But finding time to do so can be one of the biggest challenges for a CEO. Michael Porter and Nitin Nohria, Harvard Business School professor and dean, respectively, recently completed a 12-year study of CEO time management and found that CEOs spent an average of 24 percent of their working hours on electronic communications.[115]

We'd ask: Is all that time spent on email really necessary? In fact, we'd venture to say that a leader who is constantly overbooked, frantically going from one appointment to the next and struggling to find time to learn about even the most interesting perspectives, is an early indicator of a company in trouble.

In this regard, we'd recommend borrowing a page—literally—from famed investor Warren Buffett. His calendar reveals page after page with almost nothing penciled in.[116] He simply does not schedule meetings. Taking a value approach in all things, Buffett said that time is the one thing he cannot buy and he therefore cherishes it. Most business leaders can't afford to be that removed from the daily rhythm, but some go out of their way to find think time. Richard Branson recommends proactively scheduling time to dream and learn.

Making the time to learn should be a leadership necessity. When he was CEO of Microsoft, Bill Gates, for example, famously took "think weeks" each year, and he has continued to do so since stepping down from his CEO position. For each of these getaways, Gates gathers armfuls of research papers and books and heads to a secluded cabin in the Pacific Northwest. A caretaker brings him two simple meals a day, but other than that, he's alone with his reading and his thoughts. It's a way to step back from the day to day and at the same time immerse himself in topics that demand deeper concentration. These days, Gates shares books that have been especially meaningful with readers of his blog, including an annual summer reading list.

Curiosity is a crucial element in this learning mind-set. In fact, this trait is emerging as an important one in business leaders since it directly leads to new ideas and solutions. Francesca Gino, a behavioral scientist and the Tandon Family Professor of Business Administration at Harvard Business School, studied the effects of curiosity and found that it materially contributed to fewer decision-making errors, better collaboration, and improved performance.[117]

This idea is foundational at Amazon. "Our customers' needs evolve and grow, so continuous learning is an imperative for all Amazonians. We capture this intent in our leadership principle, 'Learn and Be Curious,'" said Beth Galetti, who leads HR at Amazon. "Leaders are never done learning and always seek to improve themselves. They are curious about new possibilities and act to explore them. This principle is very important because we are frequently doing things that have never been done before. Since there is often no playbook to teach nor experts to follow, we empower people to try new things and learn along the way."

A dedication to learning is especially important when it comes to technology. It's no longer practical for CEOs, CFOs, chief strategy officers, and other executives to leave technology to CIOs alone. Tech is an integral part of any true digital transformation, making it a core element of business strategy and core operations.[118] That means executives must become as comfortable with technology as they are with more familiar topics such as finance.

When Risto Siilasmaa, chairman of Nokia, wanted to get a better handle on artificial intelligence and machine learning, he rolled up his sleeves and embarked on a serious self-designed learning journey to truly understand these important areas. He started with an online course taught by AI pioneer Andrew Ng and has now taken four courses with Ng. He also read numerous books, research papers, and articles on machine learning architectures and algorithms. These days Siilasmaa is confident enough to give lectures on the subject. Besides the personal satisfaction, Nokia's chairman is now an expert in an area of increasing importance to his company.

There's a lesson here in what each of the digital leaders mentioned in this book figured out for themselves or just knew instinctively. The ability to learn, adapt, and learn some more is a prerequisite for progress of any kind in almost any field. We've covered a lot of other themes in this book, from the need for a radically faster operating metabolism to new approaches to talent recruitment and

development, to strategies and operating models adapted to digital transformations. Every one of them is predicated on an always-on adaptive learning capability.

In a technology-fueled world where disruption is the norm, adaptive learning is the winning currency because every new insight is a chance for renewal and reinvention. That's why digital organizations have ditched the traditional office grid for a dramatically different work environment designed to encourage the power of collaboration and serendipity. It's why their workforces are organized into small and nimble teams. It's why they offer decision-making and career opportunities to their digital talent that were virtually unheard of in yesterday's hierarchical, tenure-driven companies.

"Leadership and learning are indispensable to each other."

John F. Kennedy
PRESIDENT OF THE UNITED STATES OF AMERICA

This emphasis on adaptive learning is not just a formula for empowering your organization; it lies at the heart of our own ability to grow and thrive throughout both our professional and personal lives. It makes your life richer and your digital transformation more assured.

Enjoy the journey. ∎

Parting thoughts from the authors

Arun Arora
Operator

Looking at things from a new point of view.

Recently, my wife and I took our two children on a trip to Egypt. We had a great guide and were able to tour important sites throughout the country, including the pyramids in Giza and the tomb of Seti I in Luxor. That's a pretty big deal for anyone, but for kids ages 12 and 10, it was an introduction to a slice of history that was completely new to them. Their sense of the world and their place in it was suddenly and radically expanded.

As I watched them, I realized that those moments of astonishment—when a new insight changes your understanding of how the world works— are what I crave at work and what I think others crave as well.
My best professional experiences have all been about learning, trying, failing—and starting all over again. That openness to new points of view is also what makes progress possible. It's what makes successful transformations suddenly take off.

I've been extraordinarily lucky in the learning opportunities I've had in my professional life and even more in my personal life, where my wife supports my overwhelming work demands, as she did when I prepared this book, and my children teach me again and again the importance of being able to see things from a new point of view. My advice for any CEO embarking on a transformation is to build in as many opportunities for learning as possible for themselves, their teams, and ultimately their organizations.

Peter Dahlstrom
Creator

Everyone matters—but the team matters most.

I have always been an avid fan of Formula One, especially the Scuderia Ferrari team. In the heat of a race, the Ferrari pit crew can change an entire set of tires in under two seconds, an astonishing feat. Of course, it helps that advanced design means that axles, wheel nuts, and impact wrenches
are unrecognizable compared to what they were only five years ago. In addition, Ferrari engineers gather massive amounts of data each time one of their cars makes a pit stop, and they use that data to continually shave fractions of a second off the process.

But while the analytics and the technology are important, the main driver of improvements is the meticulously coordinated teamwork of up to 20 mechanics, each focused on a different task, but collaborating seamlessly. They are drilled incessantly both in the factory and in the pit until they are able to operate perfectly and instinctively in sync.

If there's one image, therefore, that I would urge chief executives to keep in mind as they embark on their digital transformations, it would be of the perfectly calibrated teamwork of that pit crew, in which each member understands the larger goal and his or her own role within it. Technology and data matter, but success in digital transformations in the end depends on the skill, training, and attitude of the team on the ground.

Klemens Hjartar
Techie

Extreme learning and why we're on the journey.

I have been a techie since I was a young kid. I was fascinated by how things worked and would hang out with my father for hours when he was repairing the car. Later, the arrival of a Macintosh was a life-changing event for me. Now as a professional leading a global group of digital front-runners, I'm still fascinated by how things work. I spend a large portion of my time trying to stay abreast of new developments and taking in new ideas. But I've been struck, like so many of us, by how challenging it is just to keep up.

That reality has reinforced for me a great truth about our modern era, which is that the fastest learner wins. In the business world, I see firsthand how important it is to work in ways that allow you to learn faster, whether that's putting together diverse teams, working in agile ways, or bringing in customer perspectives.

But this constant pressure to stay ahead can also come at the expense of staying present with the people around us, including families and coworkers. In a world where we try to learn so fast, we also need to be present. I am eternally grateful for my family constantly reminding me of this fact. I think we all need to find this balance between extreme learning and reminding ourselves why we are embarking on this journey and what really matters to us.

Florian Wunderlich
Business Builder

The power of change and constancy.

When I was younger, I wanted to be a musician. I never became one, but music is still a great passion of mine—I listen, I collect, and I (try to) play. It's a constant source of joy and inspiration for me. What is the inspiration? The endless variations that can come from 12 tones—no matter the innovations or stylistic changes. There's real magic for me in that combination of variation and constancy.

I've been thinking a lot recently about this idea and what it means in the business world. This theme has played out from my early days in business when I helped to oversee my family's local newspaper. Back then in the mid-'90s, it seemed like digital was going to completely wipe out the media business, be it small local newspapers or global media enterprises.

So much has changed, as anyone who looks at their mobile phone or opens up their computer can see. There has been a lot of testing and learning and adapting, but at its core the values that made our family newspaper work still survive. A good story or some idea that touches you is never outdated. In my work at McKinsey— and in collaborating on *Fast Times*—it has become increasingly clear to me that change is absolutely necessary, but just as important is understanding the constants that underpin what matters in business . . . or in music.

Your thoughts

References

1 Daniel Pacthod, Kevin Sneader, and Anand Swaminathan, "Why Legacy Companies Must Reinvent—or Die," *Fortune*, September 24, 2018, http://fortune.com/2018/09/24/business-strategy-technology-mckinsey/.

2 Martin Hirt, "If you're not building an ecosystem, chances are your competitors are," McKinsey & Company, June 2018, https://www.mckinsey.com/business-functions/strategy-and-corporate-finance/our-insights/the-strategy-and-corporate-finance-blog/if-youre-not-building-an-ecosystem-chances-are-your-competitors-are.

3 Michael Chui, James Manyika, Mehdi Miremadi, Nicolaus Henke, Rita Chung, Pieter Nel, and Sankalp Malhotra, "Notes from the AI Frontier: Applications and Value of Deep Learning," McKinsey Global Institute, April 2018, https://www.mckinsey.com/featured-insights/artificial-intelligence/notes-from-the-ai-frontier-applications-and-value-of-deep-learning.

4 Oliver Fleming, Tim Fountaine, Nicolaus Henke, and Tamim Saleh, "Ten Red Flags Signaling Your Analytics Program Will Fail," McKinsey & Company, May 2018, https://www.mckinsey.com/business-functions/mckinsey-analytics/our-insights/ten-red-flags-signaling-your-analytics-program-will-fail.

5 Jürgen Meffert, Peter Breuer, and Matthias Evers, "Leading in a Disruptive World: How Companies Are Reinventing Themselves," McKinsey & Company, March 2018, https://www.mckinsey.de/publikationen/leading-in-a-disruptive-world/how-companies-are-reinventing-themselves; Fred Lambert, "DHL's StreetScooter opens second factory as it emerges as an important EV manufacturer," *Eletrek*, May 31, 2018, https://electrek.co/2018/05/31/dhl-streetscooter-second-electric-vehicle-factory/.

6 Jacques Bughin, Laura LaBerge, and Anette Mellbye, "The case for digital reinvention," McKinsey & Company, February 2017, https://www.mckinsey.com/business-functions/digital-mckinsey/our-insights/the-case-for-digital-reinvention.

7 "Building a Tech-Enabled Ecosystem: An Interview with Ping An's Jessica Tan," *McKinsey Quarterly*, December 2018, https://www.mckinsey.com/featured-insights/china/building-a-tech-enabled-ecosystem-an-interview-with-ping-ans-jessica-tan.

8 Jacques Bughin, Laura LaBerge, and Anette Mellbye, "The case for digital reinvention," McKinsey & Company, February 2017, https://www.mckinsey.com/business-functions/digital-mckinsey/our-insights/the-case-for-digital-reinvention.

9 Daniel Pacthod, Kevin Sneader, and Anand Swaminathan, "Why Legacy Companies Must Reinvent—or Die," *Fortune*, September 24, 2018, http://fortune.com/2018/09/24/business-strategy-technology-mckinsey/.

10 McKinsey & Company, "AI Adoption Advances, but Foundational Barriers Remain," November 2018, https://www.mckinsey.com/featured-insights/artificial-intelligence/ai-adoption-advances-but-foundational-barriers-remain.

11 Peter Bisson, Bryce Hall, Brian McCarthy, and Khaled Rifai, "Breaking Away: The Secrets to Scaling Analytics," McKinsey & Company, May 2018, https://www.mckinsey.com/business-functions/mckinsey-analytics/our-insights/breaking-away-the-secrets-to-scaling-analytics.

12 Nicolaus Henke, Jacques Bughin, Michael Chui, James Manyika, Tamim Saleh, Bill Wiseman, and Guru Sethupathy, "The Age of Analytics: Competing in a Data-Driven World," McKinsey Global Institute, December 2016, https://www.mckinsey.com/business-functions/mckinsey-analytics/our-insights/the-age-of-analytics-competing-in-a-data-driven-world.

13 McKinsey & Company, "A Winning Operating Model for Digital Strategy," January 2019, https://www.mckinsey.com/business-functions/digital-mckinsey/our-insights/a-winning-operating-model-for-digital-strategy.

14 In the McKinsey analysis, the team looked at the relationship between frequency and

economic performance in multiple ways. The results indicate that when these digital strategy practices are carried out more frequently, revenue and EBIT are greater. The inverse also is true: when companies carry out these practices more slowly, their revenue and EBIT performance is worse.

[15] Angus Dawson, Martin Hirt, and Jay Scanlan, "The Economic Essentials of Digital Strategy," *McKinsey Quarterly*, March 2016, http://digitalmarketing.temple.edu/wp-content/uploads /sites/200/2018/08/The-economic-essentials-of-digital-strategy.pdf.

[16] Tanguy Catlin, Jay Scanlan, and Paul Willmott, "Raising your Digital Quotient," McKinsey & Company, June 2015, https://www.mckinsey.com/business-functions/strategy-and -corporate-finance/our-insights/raising-your-digital-quotient.

[17] "The Data Disconnect," *McKinsey Quarterly Five Fifty*, https://www.mckinsey.com /business-functions/mckinsey-analytics/our-insights/five-fifty-the-data-disconnect.

[18] Nicolaus Henke, Jacques Bughin, Michael Chui, James Manyika, Tamim Saleh, Bill Wiseman, and Guru Sethupathy, "The Age of Analytics: Competing in a Data-Driven World," McKinsey Global Institute, December 2016, https://www.mckinsey.com/business-functions /mckinsey-analytics/our-insights/the-age-of-analytics-competing-in-a-data-driven-world.

[19] Sam Bourton, Johanne Lavoie, and Tiffany Vogel, "Will Artificial Intelligence Make You a Better Leader?" *McKinsey Quarterly*, April 2018, https://www.mckinsey.com/business -functions/organization/our-insights/will-artificial-intelligence-make-you-a-better-leader.

[20] Mike Berardino, "Mike Tyson explains one of his most famous quotes," November 9, 2012, *South Florida Sun Sentinel*, https://www.sun-sentinel.com/sports/fl-xpm-2012-11-09 -sfl-mike-tyson-explains-one-of-his-most-famous-quotes-20121109-story.html.

[21] McKinsey & Company, "AI Adoption Advances, but Foundational Barriers Remain," November 2018, https://www.mckinsey.com/featured-insights/artificial-intelligence /ai-adoption-advances-but-foundational-barriers-remain.

[22] Michael Bender, Nicolaus Henke, and Eric Lamarre, "The Cornerstones of Large-Scale Technology Transformation," *McKinsey Quarterly*, October 2018, https://www.mckinsey .com/business-functions/digital-mckinsey/our-insights/the-cornerstones-of-large-scale -technology-transformation.

[23] Peter Bisson, Bryce Hall, Brian McCarthy, and Khaled Rifai, "Breaking Away: The Secrets to Scaling Analytics," McKinsey & Company, May 2018, https://www.mckinsey.com/business -functions/mckinsey-analytics/our-insights/breaking-away-the-secrets-to-scaling-analytics.

[24] Eric Lamarre and Brett May, "Ten Trends Shaping the Internet of Things Business Landscape," McKinsey & Company, January 2019, https://www.mckinsey.com /business-functions/digital-mckinsey/our-insights/ten-trends-shaping-the-internet-of -things-business-landscape.

[25] Michael Bender, Nicolaus Henke, and Eric Lamarre, "The Cornerstones of Large-Scale Technology Transformation," *McKinsey Quarterly*, October 2018, https://www.mckinsey .com/business-functions/digital-mckinsey/our-insights/the-cornerstones-of-large-scale -technology-transformation.

[26] McKinsey & Company, "How Digital Reinventors Are Pulling Away from the Pack," October 2017, https://www.mckinsey.it/idee/how-digital-reinventors-are-pulling-away-from-the-pack.

[27] Crunchbase, https://www.crunchbase.com/organization/axel-springer/acquisitions /acquisitions_list#section-acquisitions.

[28] Lucinda Southern, "The Secret to Axel Springer's Success: A Diverse Digital Portfolio," *Digiday*, April 1, 2016, https://digiday.com/uk/inside-axel-springers-digital -investment-strategy/.

29 Rohit Bhapkar, Joao Dias, Erez Eizenman, Irene Floretta, and Marta Rohr, "Scaling a Transformative Culture through a Digital Factory," McKinsey & Company, May 2017, https://www.mckinsey.com/business-functions/digital-mckinsey/our-insights/scaling-a-transformative-culture-through-a-digital-factory.

30 "Staying One Step Ahead at Pixar: An Interview with Ed Catmull," *McKinsey Quarterly*, March 2016, https://www.mckinsey.com/business-functions/organization/our-insights/staying-one-step-ahead-at-pixar-an-interview-with-ed-catmull.

31 Jonathan Deakin, Laura LaBerge, and Barbara O'Beirne, "Five Moves to Make during a Digital Transformation," McKinsey & Company, April 2019, https://www.mckinsey.com/business-functions/digital-mckinsey/our-insights/five-moves-to-make-during-a-digital-transformation.

32 "Building Data-Driven Culture: An Interview with ShopRunner CEO Sam Yagan," *McKinsey Quarterly*, February 2019, https://www.mckinsey.com/business-functions/mckinsey-analytics/our-insights/building-an-innovative-data-driven-culture-an-interview-with-shoprunner-ceo-sam-yagan.

33 Yan Han, Evgeniya Makarova, Matthias Ringel, and Vanya Telpis, "Digitization, Automation, and Online Testing: The Future of Pharma Quality Control," McKinsey & Company, anuary 2019, https://www.mckinsey.com/industries/pharmaceuticals-and-medical-products/our-insights/digitization-automation-and-online-testing-the-future-of-pharma-quality-control.

34 McKenna Moore, "The King of Online Dating's 3 Innovation Tips," *Fortune*, September 25, 2018, http://fortune.com/2018/09/25/king-of-online-dating-tips-innovating-in-your-business/.

35 Madhumita Murgia, "Satya Nadella, Microsoft, on Why Robots Are the Future of Work," *Financial Times*, January 29, 2017, https://www.ft.com/content/7a03c1c2-e14d-11e6-8405-9e5580d6e5fb.

36 Taylor Soper, "In Annual Shareholder Letter, Jeff Bezos Explains Why It Will Never Be Day 2 at Amazon," GeekWire, April 12, 2017, https://www.geekwire.com/2017/full-text-annual-letter-amazon-ceo-jeff-bezos-explains-avoid-becoming-day-2-company/.

37 Peter Antman, "Growing up with agile - how the Spotify 'model' has evolved," Slideshare, March 30, 2016, https://www.slideshare.net/peterantman/growing-up-with-agile-how-the-spotify-model-has-evolved.

38 Julie Goran, Laura LaBerge, and Ramesh Srinivasan, "Culture for a Digital Age," *McKinsey Quarterly*, July 2017, https://www.mckinsey.com/business-functions/digital-mckinsey/our-insights/culture-for-a-digital-age.

39 Tanguy Catlin, Laura LaBerge, and Shannon Varney, "Digital Strategy: The Four Fights You Have to Win," *McKinsey Quarterly*, October 2018, https://www.mckinsey.com/business-functions/digital-mckinsey/our-insights/digital-strategy-the-four-fights-you-have-to-win.

40 Charles Duhigg, "What Google Learned from Its Quest to Build the Perfect Team," *New York Times Magazine*, February 25, 2016, https://www.nytimes.com/2016/02/28/magazine/what-google-learned-from-its-quest-to-build-the-perfect-team.html.

41 Justin Bariso, "Google Has an Official Process in Place for Learning from Failure—and It's Absolutely Brilliant, *Inc.*, May 14, 2018, https://www.inc.com/justin-bariso/meet-postmortem-googles-brilliant-process-tool-for-learning-from-failure.html.

42 McKinsey & Company, "How to Create an Agile Organization," October 2017, https://www.mckinsey.com/business-functions/organization/our-insights/how-to-create-an-agile-organization.

43 McKinsey & Company, "Finding Talent and Speed to Transform a Credit-Card Company into a Digital Native," December 2018, https://www.mckinsey.com/business-functions

/digital-mckinsey/our-insights/finding-talent-and-speed-to-transform-a-credit-card
-company-into-a-digital-native.

44 Benedict Sheppard, Hugo Sarrazin, Garen Kouyoumjian, and Fabricio Dore, "The Business
Value of Design," *McKinsey Quarterly*, October 2018, https://www.mckinsey.com
/business-functions/mckinsey-design/our-insights/the-business-value-of-design.

45 Benedict Sheppard, Hugo Sarrazin, Garen Kouyoumjian, and Fabricio Dore, "The Business
Value of Design," *McKinsey Quarterly*, October 2018, https://www.mckinsey.com
/business-functions/mckinsey-design/our-insights/the-business-value-of-design.

46 Benedict Sheppard, Hugo Sarrazin, Garen Kouyoumjian, and Fabricio Dore, "The Business
Value of Design," *McKinsey Quarterly*, October 2018, https://www.mckinsey.com
/business-functions/mckinsey-design/our-insights/the-business-value-of-design.

47 Numetrics analysis. Numetrics is a McKinsey analytics service.

48 Scott Keller and Mary Meaney, "Attracting and Retaining the Right Talent," McKinsey &
Company, November 2017, https://www.mckinsey.com/business-functions/organization
/our-insights/attracting-and-retaining-the-right-talent.

49 "Disruptive Forces in the Industrial Sectors," Global Executive Survey, McKinsey & Company,
March 2018, https://www.mckinsey.com/~/media/McKinsey/Industries/Automotive%20
and%20Assembly/Our%20Insights/How%20industrial%20companies%20can%20
respond%20to%20disruptive%20forces/Disruptive-forces-in-the-industrial-sectors.ashx.

50 McKinsey & Company, "AI Adoption Advances, but Foundational Barriers Remain,"
November 2018, https://www.mckinsey.com/featured-insights/artificial-intelligence
/ai-adoption-advances-but-foundational-barriers-remain.

51 McKinsey & Company, "Unlocking Success in Digital Transformations," October 2018,
https://www.mckinsey.com/business-functions/organization/our-insights/unlocking
-success-in-digital-transformations.

52 Nicolaus Henke, Jacques Bughin, Michael Chui, James Manyika, Tamim Saleh, Bill Wiseman,
and Guru Sethupathy, "The Age of Analytics: Competing in a Data-Driven World," McKinsey
Global Institute, December 2016, https://www.mckinsey.com/business-functions
/mckinsey-analytics/our-insights/the-age-of-analytics-competing-in-a-data-driven-world.

53 McKinsey & Company, "Unlocking Success in Digital Transformations," October 2018,
https://www.mckinsey.com/business-functions/organization/our-insights/unlocking
-success-in-digital-transformations.

54 Wan-Lae Cheng, Thomas Dohrmann, and Jonathan Law, "The AI Factor in Talent
Management: An Interview with Catalyte's Jacob Hsu and Mike Rosenbaum," McKinsey &
Company, September 2018, https://www.mckinsey.com/industries/public-sector/our
-insights/the-ai-factor-in-talent-management-an-interview-with-catalytes-jacob-hsu-and
-mike-rosenbaum.

55 Nicolaus Henke, Jacques Bughin, Michael Chui, James Manyika, Tamim Saleh, Bill Wiseman,
and Guru Sethupathy, "The Age of Analytics: Competing in a Data-Driven World," McKinsey
Global Institute, December 2016, https://www.mckinsey.com/business-functions
/mckinsey-analytics/our-insights/the-age-of-analytics-competing-in-a-data-driven-world.

56 James Manyika, Michael Chui, Brad Brown, Jacques Bughin, Richard Dobbs, Charles
Roxburgh, and Angela Hung Byers, "Big Data: The Next Frontier for Innovation, Competition,
and Productivity," McKinsey Global Institute, May 2011, https://www.mckinsey.com
/business-functions/digital-mckinsey/our-insights/big-data-the-next-frontier-for-innovation;
the Conference Board and McKinsey & Company; State of Human Capital Survey, 2012.

57 Pablo Illanes, Susan Lund, Mona Mourshed, Scott Rutherford, and Magnus Tyreman,

"Retraining and reskilling workers in the age of automation," McKinsey Global Institute, January 2018, https://www.mckinsey.com/featured-insights/future-of-work/retraining-and-reskilling-workers-in-the-age-of-automation.

58 Pablo Illanes, Susan Lund, Mona Mourshed, Scott Rutherford, and Magnus Tyreman, "Retraining and reskilling workers in the age of automation," McKinsey Global Institute, January 2018, https://www.mckinsey.com/featured-insights/future-of-work/retraining-and-reskilling-workers-in-the-age-of-automation.

59 Tanya Staples, "Introducing the 2018 Workplace Learning Report: Talent Development's New Role in Today's Economy," LinkedIn: The Learning Blog, February 27, 2018, https://learning.linkedin.com/blog/learning-thought-leadership/introducing-the-2018-workplace-learning-report--talent-developme.

60 Ramona Schindelheim, "Shaping the Future Workforce: AT&T's Chief Learning Officer Helps Instill Culture of Lifelong Learning," WorkingNation, January 29, 2018, https://workingnation.com/shaping-future-workforce-john-palmer/.

61 John Donovan and Cathy Benko, "AT&T's Talent Overhaul," *Harvard Business Review*, October 1, 2016, https://hbr.org/product/at-t-s-talent-overhaul/R1610E-PDF-JPN?referral=03069.

62 Matt Deimund, Michael Drory, Daniel Law, and Maria Valdivieso, "The Five Things Sales-Growth Winners Do to Invest in Their People," McKinsey & Company, October 2018, https://www.mckinsey.com/business-functions/marketing-and-sales/our-insights/the-five-things-sales-growth-winners-do-to-invest-in-their-people.

63 Richard Benson-Armer, Arne Gast, and Nick van Dam, "Learning at the Speed of Business," *McKinsey Quarterly*, May 2016, https://www.mckinsey.com/business-functions/organization/our-insights/learning-at-the-speed-of-business.

64 Julie DeLoyd, Maria Valdivieso, Ben Vonwiller, and Michael Viertler, "For Top Sales-Force Performance, Treat Your Reps like Customers," McKinsey & Company, June 2017, https://www.mckinsey.com/business-functions/marketing-and-sales/our-insights/for-top-sales-force-performance-treat-your-reps-like-customers.

65 Jenifer Robertson, "How to Build a Culture of Learning," AT&T Technology Blog, May 24, 2018, https://about.att.com/innovationblog/culture_of_learning.

66 Bertil Chappuis, Steve Reis, Maria Valdivieso De Uster, and Michael Viertler, "Boosting Your Sales ROI: How Digital and Analytics Can Drive New Performance and Growth," McKinsey & Company, February 2018, https://www.mckinsey.com/business-functions/marketing-and-sales/our-insights/boosting-your-sales-roi.

67 Emily Ross, Bill Schaninger, and Emily Seng Yue, "How to Advance Your Talent Plan to Stay Relevant," McKinsey & Company, August 27, 2018, https://www.mckinsey.com/business-functions/organization/our-insights/the-organization-blog/how-to-advance-your-talent-plan-to-stay-relevant.

68 Stackoverflow.com 2018 survey.

69 RiseSmart, "The Connection between HR Analytics and Employer Brand: Are You Using Big Data to Manage Your Employer Brand?," https://info.risesmart.com/wp-rg-insight-whitepaper.

70 Scott Keller and Mary Meaney, "Attracting and Retaining the Right Talent," McKinsey & Company, November 2017, https://www.mckinsey.com/business-functions/organization/our-insights/attracting-and-retaining-the-right-talent.

71 Oliver Fleming, Tim Fountaine, Nicolaus Henke, and Tamim Saleh, "Ten Red Flags Signaling Your Analytics Program Will Fail," McKinsey & Company, May 2018, https://www.mckinsey.com/business-functions/mckinsey-analytics/our-insights/ten-red-flags-signaling-your-analytics-program-will-fail.

72 The competitive advantages that companies stand to gain by creating homegrown applications have all but disappeared in most sectors. There are, however, certain sectors where proprietary applications can still add value. These are mainly sectors whose core functions must be executed in real time, such as securities trading.

73 McKinsey & Company, "IT's Future Value Proposition," July 2017, https://www.mckinsey .com/business-functions/digital-mckinsey/our-insights/its-future-value-proposition.

74 McKinsey & Company, "AI Adoption Advances, but Foundational Barriers Remain," November 2018, https://www.mckinsey.com/featured-insights/artificial-intelligence /ai-adoption-advances-but-foundational-barriers-remain.

75 McKinsey & Company, "A Winning Operating Model for Digital Strategy," January 2019, https://www.mckinsey.com/business-functions/digital-mckinsey/our-insights /a-winning-operating-model-for-digital-strategy.

76 McKinsey & Company, "A Winning Operating Model for Digital Strategy," January 2019, https://www.mckinsey.com/business-functions/digital-mckinsey/our-insights /a-winning-operating-model-for-digital-strategy.

77 "Can IT rise to the digital challenge?" McKinsey & Company, October 2018, https://www.mckinsey.com/business-functions/digital-mckinsey/our-insights /can-it-rise-to-the-digital-challenge.

78 Although it is advantageous to hire digital talent on a permanent basis, some companies will want to bring in contractors or short-term hires to plug any serious digital-talent gaps in the early stages of their digital transformations, when they want to develop new solutions but don't yet have the personnel to do so.

79 "Can IT rise to the digital challenge?" McKinsey & Company, October 2018, https://www.mckinsey.com/business-functions/digital-mckinsey/our-insights /can-it-rise-to-the-digital-challenge.

80 Based on data from the Global State of Online Digital Trust Survey and Index 2018 from CA Technologies, https://www.ca.com/us/collateral/white-papers/the-global-state-of -online-digital-trust.html.

81 Digital Transformation Security Global Survey, 2016, https://www.oneidentity.com /whitepaper/global-survey-digital-transformation-security-survey8113164/.

82 While developers are ordinarily assisted by release-management teams, the team or sometimes even the developer bears ultimate responsibility for putting code into the release "machine" or taking out faulty code when it malfunctions.

83 "2017 Data Breach Investigations Report (DBIR) from the Perspective of Exterior Security Perimeter," Verizon, July 26, 2017, https://www.verizondigitalmedia.com /blog/2017/07/2017-verizon-data-breach-investigations-report/.

84 Tessa Basford and Bill Schaninger, "The four building blocks of change," *McKinsey Quarterly*, April 2016, https://www.mckinsey.com/business-functions/organization/our -insights/the-four-building-blocks--of-change

85 McKinsey & Company, "Unlocking Success in Digital Transformations," October 2018, https://www.mckinsey.com/business-functions/organization/our-insights/unlocking -success-in-digital-transformations.

86 "2017 America's Most Admired Knowledge Enterprises (MAKE) Report," http://www.cewd.org/documents/2017AmericasMAKE-ExecutiveSummary.pdf.

87 McKinsey & Company, "How to Create an Agile Organization," October 2017, https://www.mckinsey.com/business-functions/organization/our-insights /how-to-create-an-agile-organization.

149

[88] As of March 26, 2019, Uber had reached an agreement to acquire Careem for $3.1 billion, making it the first tech "unicorn" in the Middle East.

[89] McKinsey & Company, "Unlocking Success in Digital Transformations," October 2018, https://www.mckinsey.com/business-functions/organization/our-insights/unlocking-success-in-digital-transformations.

[90] "Winning with Talent," McKinsey & Company research, 2017.

[91] Jonathan Deakin, Laura LaBerge, and Barbara O'Beirne, "Five Moves to Make during a Digital Transformation," McKinsey & Company, April 2019, https://www.mckinsey.com/business-functions/digital-mckinsey/our-insights/five-moves-to-make-during-a-digital-transformation.

[92] Jonathan Deakin, Laura LaBerge, and Barbara O'Beirne, "Five Moves to Make during a Digital Transformation," McKinsey & Company, April 2019, https://www.mckinsey.com/business-functions/digital-mckinsey/our-insights/five-moves-to-make-during-a-digital-transformation.

[93] Jacques Bughin, Tanguy Catlin, and Laura LaBerge, "How Digital Reinventors Are Pulling Away from the Pack," McKinsey & Company, October 27, 2017, https://www.mckinsey.com/business-functions/digital-mckinsey/our-insights/how-digital-reinventors-are-pulling-away-from-the-pack.

[94] Jacques Bughin, Tanguy Catlin, and Laura LaBerge, "How Digital Reinventors Are Pulling Away from the Pack," McKinsey & Company, October 27, 2017, https://www.mckinsey.com/business-functions/digital-mckinsey/our-insights/how-digital-reinventors-are-pulling-away-from-the-pack.

[95] Jacques Bughin, Tanguy Catlin, and Laura LaBerge, "How Digital Reinventors Are Pulling Away from the Pack," McKinsey & Company, October 27, 2017, https://www.mckinsey.com/business-functions/digital-mckinsey/our-insights/how-digital-reinventors-are-pulling-away-from-the-pack.

[96] Richard Branson, "My Top 10 Quotes on Communication," Virgin, May 11, 2015, https://www.virgin.com/richard-branson/my-top-10-quotes-on-communication.

[97] David Beaumont, Joël Thibert, and Jonathan Tilley, "Same Lean Song, Different Transformation Tempo," McKinsey & Company, September 2017, https://www.mckinsey.com/business-functions/operations/our-insights/same-lean-song-different-transformation-tempo.

[98] David Beaumont, Joël Thibert, and Jonathan Tilley, "Same Lean Song, Different Transformation Tempo," McKinsey & Company, September 2017, https://www.mckinsey.com/business-functions/operations/our-insights/same-lean-song-different-transformation-tempo.

[99] David Beaumont, Joël Thibert, and Jonathan Tilley, "Same Lean Song, Different Transformation Tempo," McKinsey & Company, September 2017, https://www.mckinsey.com/business-functions/operations/our-insights/same-lean-song-different-transformation-tempo.

[100] Peter Breuer and Gemma D'Auria, "Reshaping 'Retailtainment' in the Middle East and Beyond," McKinsey & Company, August 2017, https://www.mckinsey.com/industries/retail/our-insights/reshaping-retail-tainment-in-the-middle-east-and-beyond.

[101] Marguerite Ward, "Why PepsiCo CEO Indra Nooyi Writes Letters to Her Employees' Parents," CNBC, February 1, 2017, https://www.cnbc.com/2017/02/01/why-pepsico-ceo-indra-nooyi-writes-letters-to-her-employees-parents.html.

[102] Ali Montag, "Jeff Bezos' First Desk at Amazon Was a Door with Four-by-Fours for Legs—Here's Why It Still Is Today," CNBC, January 23, 2018, https://www.cnbc.com/2018/01/23/jeff-bezos-first-desk-at-amazon-was-made-of-a-wooden-door.html.

[103] Andrew Hill, "Can Microsoft's Chief Satya Nadella Restore It to Glory?" *Financial Times*,

October 13, 2017, https://www.ft.com/content/081b2240-ae7e-11e7-aab9-abaa44b1e130.

104 Roger Bannister, "Roger Bannister: 'The Day I Broke the Four-Minute Mile,'" *Telegraph* (UK), March 30, 2014, https://www.telegraph.co.uk/sport/10731234/Roger-Bannister-The-day-I-broke-the-four-minute-mile.html.

105 Canada Pension Plan Investment Board and McKinsey & Company, "Focusing Capital on the Long Term," survey, 2016.

106 Rensselaer Polytechnic Institute, "Minority Rules: Scientists Discover Tipping Point for the Spread of Ideas", ScienceDaily, July 26, 2011, https://www.sciencedaily.com/releases/2011/07/110725190044.htm.

107 McKinsey & Company, "How the implementation of organizational change is evolving," February 2018, https://www.mckinsey.com/business-functions/mckinsey-implementation/our-insights/how-the-implementation-of-organizational-change-is-evolving.

108 Michael Bucy, Tony Fagan, Benoît Maraite, and Cornelia Piaia, "Keeping Transformations on Target," McKinsey & Company, March 10, 2017, https://www.mckinsey.it/idee/keeping-transformations-on-target.

109 McKinsey & Company, "How the implementation of organizational change is evolving," February 2018, https://www.mckinsey.com/business-functions/mckinsey-implementation/our-insights/how-the-implementation-of-organizational-change-is-evolving.

110 McKinsey & Company, "How the implementation of organizational change is evolving," February 2018, https://www.mckinsey.com/business-functions/mckinsey-implementation/our-insights/how-the-implementation-of-organizational-change-is-evolving.

111 Jacques Bughin, Tanguy Catlin, and Laura LaBerge, "How Digital Reinventors Are Pulling Away from the Pack," McKinsey & Company, October 27, 2017, https://www.mckinsey.it/idee/how-digital-reinventors-are-pulling-away-from-the-pack.

112 Dominic Barton, James Manyika, and Sarah Keohane Williamson, "Finally, Evidence That Managing for the Long Term Pays Off," Harvard Business Review, February 9, 2017, https://hbr.org/2017/02/finally-proof-that-managing-for-the-long-term-pays-off.

113 Corporate Performance Analytics; Capital IQ; McKinsey analysis.

114 Corporate Performance Analytics; Capital IQ; McKinsey analysis.

115 Michael E. Porter and Nitin Nohria, "How CEOs Manage Time," Harvard Business Review, July–August 2018, https://www.hbs.edu/faculty/Pages/item.aspx?num=54691.

116 Catherine Clifford, "What Warren Buffett Taught Bill Gates about Managing Time by Sharing His (Nearly) Blank Calendar," CNBC, September 7, 2018, http://ccare.stanford.edu/press_posts/what-warren-buffett-taught-bill-gates-about-managing-time-by-sharing-his-nearly-blank-calendar/.

117 Francesca Gino, "The Business Case for Curiosity," *Harvard Business Review*, September–October 2018, https://hbr.org/2018/09/curiosity.

118 According to McKinsey research, some distinguishing features of digital reinventors—the digital natives, incumbents competing digitally, and incumbents using digital moves to compete in new markets, which outperform traditional incumbents—are that they apply advanced technologies at scale, invest in digital more boldly, and make bigger changes to their business portfolios. For more, see "How Digital Reinventors Are Pulling Away from the Pack," October 2017, https://www.mckinsey.com/business-functions/digital-mckinsey/our-insights/how-digital-reinventors-are-pulling-away-from-the-pack.

Take the first step . . .

McKinsey.com/FastTimes